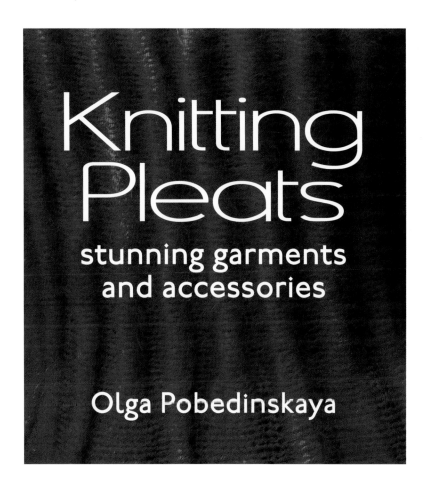

Knitting Pleats

stunning garments and accessories

Olga Pobedinskaya

Martingale®
& COMPANY

Credits

President & CEO: Tom Wierzbicki

Editorial Director: Mary V. Green

Managing Editor: Tina Cook

Developmental Editor: Karen Costello Soltys

Technical Editor: Ursula Reikes

Copy Editor: Melissa Bryan

Design Director: Stan Green

Production Manager: Regina Girard

Illustrator: Robin Strobel

Cover & Text Designer: Shelly Garrison

Photographer: Brent Kane

Mission Statement

Dedicated to providing quality products
and service to inspire creativity.

Knitting Pleats: Stunning Garments and Accessories
© 2011 by Olga Pobedinskaya

Martingale & Company
19021 120th Ave. NE, Suite 102
Bothell, WA 98011-9511
www.martingale-pub.com

The information in this book is presented in good faith, but no warranty is given nor results guaranteed. Since Martingale & Company has no control over choice of materials or procedures, the company assumes no responsibility for the use of this information.

Printed in China
16 15 14 13 12 11   8 7 6 5 4 3 2 1

Library of Congress Cataloging-in-Publication Data is available upon request.
ISBN: 978-1-60468-042-3

Dedication

In memory of my
Russian-Ukrainian grandmother,
Hristina

Contents

Introduction — 7

Understanding Knitted Pleats — 8

Useful Techniques — 11

Shoulder Chic: Beaded Top — 14

Cupola: Puffy Pleats Hat — 17

Curly Confection: Puffy Pleats Scarf — 19

Pagoda: Pleated Beret — 22

Concert: Concertina Bag — 25

Accordion: Vertical Pleats Bag — 28

Golden Fleece: Vicuña Collar — 30

Silver Darts: Sectional Pleats T-Shirt — 34

Ribbons and Ties: Sweet Pleated-Neck Bolero — 38

Wings: Butterfly Shawl — 42

Vested Interest: Pleated-Back Vest — 45

Fanned: Three-Fan Shawl — 48

Borderlines: Pleated-Trim Jacket — 52

Eve's Ribs: Horizontal Ribbed Pullover — 56

Long Way Back: Elongated-Back Pullover — 61

Lipstick Glamour: Top with Vertical Pleats — 65

Grace of Grays: Short-Row Pleats Pullover — 70

Abbreviations and Glossary — 77

Resources — 78

Acknowledgments — 79

Introduction

My Russian-Ukrainian grandmother, Hristina, who died in May 2008 at the age of 95, knew how to do everything: spin yarns (both literally and metaphorically!), weave, sew, knit, crochet, embroider, dress leather, build shacks and fences, paint murals, keep animals, plant orchards and kitchen gardens, and she even made moonshine vodka, strangely reminiscent—as I would later discover to my surprise—of Japanese sake. She lived in a Russian village south of Voronezh. I spent most of my early childhood and all my school vacations with her.

She was the one who first introduced me to knitting. I close my eyes and see her with a sock in the making, commenting that the yarn is soft, but could be a little less waxy. And we would laugh together at the socks our neighbor was making—they were as stiff as a board! Or my grandmother would be knitting a traditional gray shawl of fine goat yarn, using bicycle spokes with bent ends (no circular needles back then!), and she would teach me to work a basic lace border. I was only allowed to knit for dolls. I couldn't wait to get my hands on all those yarns, especially the wonderful Angora rabbit yarn that refused to cling to base threads, but which could eventually be knitted into something ethereal and cloud-like. Only at about age 9 or 10 was I finally allowed to help out with shawl knitting, and from that day on knitting became both my favorite pastime and a necessary source of income for the family. I took my turn, following in the footsteps of my aunt and my mother, in learning the craft that was passed on from generation to generation without written patterns. There were no knitting books or magazines to be had, but I was an avid reader, and the village had a surprisingly good library, full of classics of Russian, Western, and Eastern literature as well as encyclopedias. From these sources I could glean some idea of other worlds, other cultures, other fashions.

The Russian-Ukrainian folk dresses that I saw during my childhood in the countryside were one of the inspirations for the pleated designs in this book. The library and my summer reading there led to another major influence—my early, and enduring, fascination with Japanese culture. Japanese movies, along with children's television programs about origami and ikebana, fed that interest, until I was eventually able to view Japanese art in Moscow and St. Petersburg museums. Later, when I moved to the West, I continued my journey of discovery and was fortunate enough to make friends with a Japanese family, highlighted by a visit with them in Japan in 1998. Somehow, for me at least, the Japanese traditions of patterns based on geometry translate naturally into knitting. The unusual creations of Japanese fashion designers—Rei Kawakubo, Yoshi Yamamoto, and Issey Miyake—provided the main inspiration for the designs presented here.

If this book embodies to some extent an expression of advanced knitting, it is not because the projects are particularly difficult to knit, for they are not, but because they represent the creative combination of different cultural traditions. Perhaps this is a particularly Russian phenomenon—borrowing from other cultures, combining these influences with one's own culture (which is already a hybrid anyway), and producing a new twist, to make something new and fresh out of acknowledged origins.

This collection of original, sophisticated designs is based on the somewhat neglected techniques of pleats and folds. Fashion catwalks are at present exhibiting many amazing pieces of knitwear using pleats, and this book will not only offer you the chance to create your own pieces of knitting couture but will also inspire you to invent your own fashion statements.

The projects are arranged in order of difficulty. For best results use the yarns recommended here, but substitution is possible as long as the gauge is achieved. When using hand-dyed yarns, it's best to alternate different skeins every two rows, four rows, or any number of rounds.

Pleats are simple enough and open up fascinating knitting and designing possibilities for the average knitter. Before starting a project, I recommend that you read this section to gain an understanding of how the pleats are worked. Additional knitting techniques used in the projects can be found on pages 11–13.

BASIC PLEATS

Pleats are worked horizontally in the knitting, and they can be made either across an entire row or on only a section of a row. Look closely at the photo below and you'll see a series of pleats separated by rows of knitting.

Close-up of pleats

A pleat is formed by working a given number of rows, and then joining the live stitches on the needle along with stitches picked up from a specific row below. Stitches are picked up on the wrong side of the designated row using a spare needle, one slightly smaller than the one used for the knitting. Insert the needle under a stitch and leave the stitch on the needle. Continue to pick up the stitches (either across a row or on only a section as indicated) and leave them on the needle.

Picking up stitches on the wrong side

Holding the main needle and the spare needle with picked-up stitches in your left hand, knit together one stitch from each needle. This is similar to working a three-needle bind-off, but you don't bind off!

Joining the pleat

Full-Row Pleats in Stockinette Stitch

These pleats are worked across an entire row of knitting. Work the required number of rows, and then follow the instructions in the preceding paragraphs and pick up stitches for the pleat across the entire row. To help you identify the row on which to pick up the stitches, place a removable marker in the first stitch and the last stitch of the row. Be sure to pick up those stitches where the markers were placed.

Full-row pleats worked across the entire row

Sectional Pleats in Stockinette Stitch

These pleats are worked on a section of a row, either at one end or somewhere in the middle. To identify the section to be pleated, place markers on the wrong side in the first and last stitches of the pleat. The instruction for the following sample would be "P3, place removable marker, P10, place removable marker, P3." Place the markers as follows: After you work the first stitch of the P10, place the removable marker in that stitch. Work the remaining nine stitches, and after you've worked the last stitch of the P10, place the marker in that stitch.

Removable markers in first stitch
and last stitch of a sectional pleat

After you knit the designated number of rows, join the pleat on the next right-side row. Pick up stitches in the same manner as for the full-row pleats, except pick up only the stitches between the removable markers.

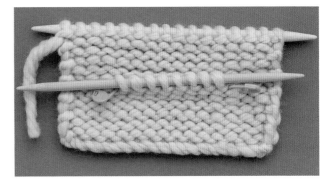

Pick up stitches between removable markers.

To join the pleat, knit to the first marker, and then knit together one stitch from each needle until all picked-up stitches are used. Knit the remaining stitches on the left needle.

Joining a sectional pleat

The result is a sectional pleat that shapes the knitted piece, similar to darts in dressmaking.

A completed sectional pleat

Sectional Pleats in Horizontal Ribbing

Pleats can be incorporated into dimensional stripes of stockinette stitch and reverse stockinette stitch. Work the required rows in stockinette stitch, and on the last row of the stockinette stitch place markers to indicate the beginning and end of the pleat. Work the required rows in reverse stockinette stitch.

Removable markers indicate the beg and end of the pleat.

With a spare needle, pick up the stitches on the wrong side between the markers. To join the pleat, change to stockinette stitch and knit to the first marker, then knit together one stitch from each needle until all picked-up stitches are used. Knit the remaining stitches on the left needle.

Joining the reverse stockinette stitch pleat

Pleats in reverse stockinette stitch appear rounded.

Puffy Pleats

Puffy pleats are worked in a similar manner, but the stitches within the rows that form the pleat are doubled. Stitches are doubled on the second row of the pleat, and then decreased to the original number on the last row of the pleat. See Cupola: Puffy Pleats Hat on page 17 and Curly Confection: Puffy Pleats Scarf on page 19.

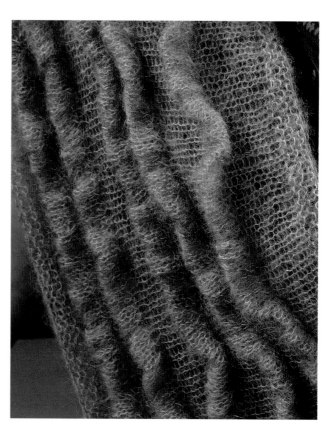

An example of puffy pleats (see page 19)

If one of the projects includes an unfamiliar technique, the following instructions will help you master it.

SHORT ROWS

Fan-shaped pieces are made by knitting only a part of a row, and then turning and wrapping a stitch to avoid holes. This short-row technique might be a little different from what you are used to working. Read the directions carefully and then give it a try. You'll find that it is easy to do.

To work short rows, work the required number of stitches in the pattern, and then turn the work so that the wrong side is facing you. With the yarn in back, slip the last stitch worked purlwise, and bring the yarn to the front. The yarn is now wrapped around the slipped stitch.

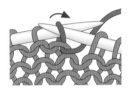 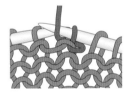

Finish the wrong-side row, and turn to face the right side. On the next right-side row, work to the wrapped stitch, slip the wrapped stitch onto the right-hand needle purlwise.

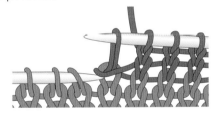

Use the left-hand needle to pick up the wrap and put it on the left-hand needle, transfer the wrapped stitch back to the left-hand needle, and work the wrap and the wrapped stitch together.

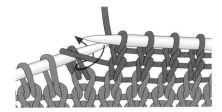

REVERSE STOCKINETTE STITCH BOBBLES

Bobbles are clever little additions that are easy to make. Work to the spot indicated in the pattern for the bobble. To make a bobble, (K1, YO, K1, YO, K1) all into the same stitch making five stitches out of one.

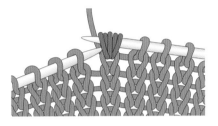

Turn and K5, turn and P5, turn and K5.

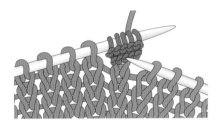

Turn and knit the five stitches together through the back loops; finish the row.

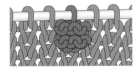

INCREASES

Two different increases are used for the patterns in this book.

Make One Stitch (M1)

Work up to the point where the increase is supposed to be. Pick up the horizontal strand between the stitch just worked and the next stitch by inserting the left needle from front to back and placing the strand onto the left needle. Now, knit this stitch through the back loop.

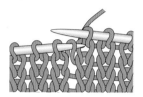 

Knit One in Front and Back (K1f&b)

Knit into the stitch you want to increase in as you normally would, but do not take the stitch off either needle. Bring the right needle around to the back of your work and knit that same stitch through the back loop of the stitch. Slip the stitch off the left needle.

Purl One in Front and Back (P1f&b)

Purl into the designated stitch but do not take the stitch off of either needle. Bring the right needle around to the back of your work and insert it into the back of the stitch from left to right and purl again. Slip the stitch off the needle.

DECREASES

When the instructions call for decreases at each end of a row, work K2tog at the beginning of the row and ssk at the end of right-side rows. Use P2tog at the beginning and end of wrong-side rows.

Knit Two Stitches Together (K2tog)

Insert the right needle from left to right through the second stitch and then the first stitch on the left hand needle and knit them as one stitch.

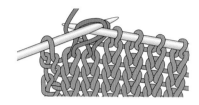

Slip, Slip, Knit (ssk)

Slip the next two stitches individually as if to knit onto the right-hand needle. Insert the left-hand needle into the front of the stitches and knit these two stitches together through the back loops, making one stitch out of two.

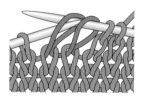 

Slip two stitches to right needle.   Knit two stitches together.

Purl Two Together (P2tog)

Insert the right needle from right to left through the first and second stitches on the left-hand needle and purl them as one stitch.

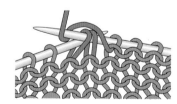

SEAMS

If you're new to any of the seaming techniques used in the projects, refer to the following instructions.

Bound-Off Edge to Bound-Off Edge

Use this method to sew the shoulders together and re-create a row of knitting. Place one bound-off edge above the other bound-off edge. With right side facing you and tapestry needle threaded with yarn, attach the yarn to the upper edge. Bring the needle under the bottom edge and pull it out to the right side through the middle of the first stitch. *Insert the needle under both sides of the first stitch on the upper edge. Return to the middle of the first stitch on the bottom edge, and pull the needle out in the middle of the second stitch on the bottom edge. Repeat from * across all stitches. Pull yarn gently and evenly. Do not pull too tight. The stitches should look like a row of knitting.

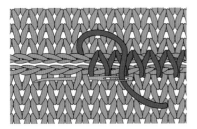

Vertical Edge to Vertical Edge (Mattress Stitch)

Use this method to sew side seams together. Place edges to be sewn parallel to each other. With right side facing you and tapestry needle threaded with yarn, attach yarn to the bottom of the left piece. Insert the needle in the first stitch on the right piece and bring it up in the first space. Insert the needle under the horizontal bar between the first and second stitches of the right piece, and pull thread through. *Insert the needle under two horizontal bars on the alternate side and pull

thread through. Repeat from * for the length of the seam. Pull the yarn tight to conceal the stitches.

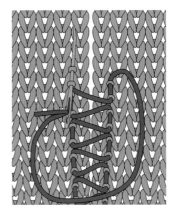

Vertical Edge to Bound-Off Edge

Use this method to sew a sleeve into an armhole edge. Work the stitches on the sleeve as in "Bound-off Edge to Bound-off Edge." Work the stitches on the armhole edge as in "Vertical Edge to Vertical Edge." The edges should match without distorting or stretching the stitches. You may need to adjust the number of bars you go under on the vertical edge, alternating one bar and two bars as needed.

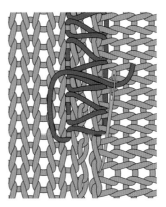

Curved edges require particular care, but the basic principles remain the same as above: The actual seam is worked into the space one stitch from the edges of each piece being put together. So the first stitch of each edge is not used and goes on the wrong side. No part of the seam should be distorted or stretched.

BLOCKING

Blocking can be achieved by steaming or spraying the pieces with water and laying flat to the desired measurements. Let dry completely. The only pleats that need steaming are the horizontal shaped pleats in Concert: Concertina Bag (page 25) and Pagoda: Pleated Beret (page 22).

SHOULDER CHIC: Beaded Top

This simple, yet sophisticated, design brings out the very best in this beautiful yarn, and looks lovely on bare shoulders.

Skill Level: Easy ◖■☐☐

Sizes: Small (Medium, Large)

Finished Length: 12½ (13½, 14½)"

Finished Bust Measurement: 36 (38, 40)"

MATERIALS

3 (4, 4) skeins of Beaded Lace from Tilli Tomas (100% silk with petite beads; 50 g; 168 yds) in color 72 Black Cherry (**3**)

US 7 (4.5 mm) straight or circular needle (24" long)

Spare US 4 (3.5 mm) needle to pick up stitches

2 removable stitch markers

GAUGE

20 sts and 21 rows = 4" in St st

FEATURED TECHNIQUE

"Sectional Pleats in Stockinette Stitch" on page 9.

FRONT AND BACK (MAKE 2.)

A group of sectional pleats in two different lengths are featured on the front and back.

CO 90 (96, 102) sts.

Work in St st with 3-st garter border at each end.

Row 1: Knit.

Row 2: K3, purl to last 3 sts, K3.

Row 3: Knit.

Row 4: K3, P32 (35, 38), place removable marker, P20, place removable marker, P32 (35, 38), K3.

Rows 5–8: Work in established patt.

Row 9: K35 (38, 41), join pleat with 20 sts picked up from row 4 between markers, K35 (38, 41). Remove markers.

Rows 10–13: Work in established patt.

Row 14: K3, P28 (31, 34), place removable marker, P28, place removable marker, P28 (31, 34), K3.

Rows 15–18: Work in established patt.

Row 19: K31 (34, 37), join pleat with 28 sts picked up from row 14 between markers, K31 (34, 37). Remove markers.

For Small
Rep rows 2–19 twice.

For Medium
Rep rows 2–19 twice and rows 2–9 once.

For Large
Rep rows 2–19 three times.

For all sizes
Work row 2 once.

BO all sts loosely.

FINISHING

Sew tog 5 (5½, 6)" of BO edge on each side for shoulders. Sew tog 5 (6, 7)" for side seams.

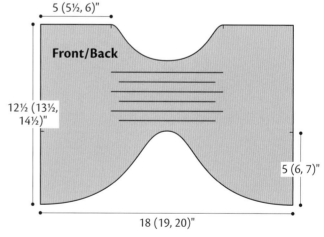

5 (5½, 6)"

Front/Back

12½ (13½, 14½)"

5 (6, 7)"

18 (19, 20)"

CUPOLA: Puffy Pleats Hat

This design shows a variation on simple horizontal pleats. The irregular wavy effect is created by doubling the number of stitches in parts of the pleats. This hat also looks great in multicolored yarns.

Skill Level: Intermediate ◼◼◼◻

Finished Circumference: Approx 22"

MATERIALS

Lush by Classic Elite Yarns (50% angora, 50% wool; 50 g; 124 yds) 🄸

MC 2 skeins in color 4413

CC 1 skein in color 4401

US 8 (5 mm) needles

Spare US 5 (3.75 mm) needle to pick up stitches

1 stitch marker

Tapestry needle

GAUGE

20 sts and 32 rows = 4" in garter st

FEATURED TECHNIQUES

"Full-Row Pleats in Stockinette Stitch" on page 9.

"Puffy Pleats" on page 10.

The hat is worked sideways, back and forth in rows, and then seamed. It is worked in garter st with puffy pleats in St st.

BACKGROUND

With MC, CO 42 sts.

Rows 1–3: Knit.

Rows 4 and 5: K22, turn, wrap, knit to end.

Row 6: Knit, working wrap and wrapped st tog.

Rows 7–9: Knit.

Rows 10 and 11: K32, turn, wrap, knit to end.

Row 12: Knit, working wrap and wrapped st tog.

Rep rows 1–12 once and rows 1–6 once.

CONTRASTING-COLOR PLEAT

Change to CC, do not cut MC. Work pleat as follows.

Row 1: K20, place removable marker, knit to end.

Row 2: P1f&b in each st to marker, sm, purl to end—62 sts.

Rows 3–9: Work in St st.

Row 10: P2tog to marker, remove marker, purl to end—42 sts.

Row 11: Change to MC, do not cut CC, join pleat across sts picked up from last row of MC.

Work background (beg with row 2) and contrasting-color pleat another 6 times for a total of 7 reps.

BO all sts.

FINISHING

Sew tog CO and BO edge. Thread tapestry needle with 2 strands of MC and with RS facing you, weave yarn in and out of top edge of hat along background, avoiding pleats. Gather, pull ends tog, and tie in a knot. Pull ends to WS and weave in. Do not press or steam.

CURLY CONFECTION:
Puffy Pleats Scarf

Show off your style while staying snug and warm. Puffy pleats look fabulous in soft, lightweight kid mohair. The shape of these pleats reminds me of a candy bar called Curly Wurly, popular in parts of Europe; with this great scarf wrapped around your shoulders, you'll look sweetly scrumptious yourself.

Skill Level: Intermediate ◼◼◼◻

Finished Measurements: Approx 11" x 74"

MATERIALS

4 balls of Kid-Seta from Schulana (70% kid mohair, 30% silk; 25 g; 210 m) in color 108 (3)

US 7 (4.5 mm) circular needle (36" long)

Spare US 6 (4.25 mm) circular needle (32" long) to pick up stitches

US 10 (6 mm) needle to CO and BO

20 removable stitch markers

GAUGE

14½ sts and 27 rows = 4" in St st on larger needle

FEATURED TECHNIQUES

"Sectional Pleats in Stockinette Stitch" on page 9.

"Puffy Pleats" on page 10.

SCARF

Because the pleats are very long, it is helpful to place several removable markers between the first marker and the last marker of the pleat. This will help you pick up stitches later across the correct row.

With size 10 needle, CO 240 sts.

Change to size 7 needle.

Rows 1–6: Work in garter st for border.

Change to St st with 4-st garter border at each end.

Row 7: Knit.

Row 8: K4, purl to last 4 sts, K4.

Rows 9–17: Work as established.

Row 18: K4, P26, place removable marker, purl across row adding a few more removable markers (one approx every 20 sts) to last 30 sts, place removable marker, P26, K4.

Row 19: K4, K26, K1f&b in each st to last 30 sts (180 times), K26, K4—420 sts.

Rows 20–27: Work as established.

Row 28: K4, P26, P2tog to last marker (180 times), P26, K4—240 sts.

With size 6 needle and WS facing, pick up sts between first and last markers from row 18.

Row 29: K4, K26, join pleat with sts picked up from row 18 between first and last markers, K26, K4.

Rows 30–39: Work as established.

Row 40: K4, P36, place removable marker, purl across row adding a few more removable markers to last 40 sts, place removable marker, P36, K4.

Row 41: K4, K36, K1f&b in each st to last 40 sts (160 times), K36, K4—400 sts.

Rows 42–49: Work as established.

Row 50: K4, P36, P2tog to last marker (160 times), P36, K4—240 sts.

Row 51: K4, K36, join pleat with sts picked up from row 40 between first and last markers, K36, K4.

Rows 52–61: Work as established.

Rep rows 18–61 once, and then rep rows 18–40 once, omitting markers on row 40.

Work 6 rows in garter st for border.

BO loosely with size 10 needle.

FINISHING

Weave in ends. Steam edges lightly.

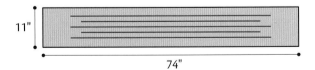

PAGODA: Pleated Beret

This beret is worked in stockinette stitch and shaped by simple increases and decreases, creating a captivating hat for the fall season.

Skill Level: Easy ◼◼◻◻

Finished Circumference: Approx 18" at band

MATERIALS

Zara from Filatura di Crosa (100% merino wool; 50 g/1.75 oz; 136.5 yds/125 m) ③

A   2 skeins in color 1663

B   1 skein in color 1493

C   1 skein in color 1503

US 7 (4.5 mm) circular needles (16" and 24" long)

Set of US 7 (4.5 mm) double-pointed needles

1 stitch marker

GAUGE

21 sts and 31 rows = 4" in St st

BAND

With A, CO 7 sts.

Work in K1, P1 ribbing with sl-st edges as follows.

Row 1 (RS): Sl 1 pw, K1, P1, K1, P1, K2.

Row 2: Sl 1 pw, P1, K1, P1, K1, P1, K1.

Rep rows 1 and 2 until piece measures 18" (approx 132 rows). BO all sts. Fasten off.

Sew tog CO and BO edges of band. Rejoin yarn to CO end. With A and 16"-long circular needle, PU 66 sts along the RS edge with the CO tail. Join, pm, and knit 1 rnd.

BOTTOM PLEAT

Rnd 1: (K1, K1f&b) around—99 sts.

Knit all rnds even, except for the following rnds:

Rnd 5: (K2, K1f&b) around—132 sts.

Rnd 11: (K3, K1f&b) around—165 sts.

Change to 24"-long circular needle.

Rnd 19: (K4, K1f&b) around—198 sts.

Rnd 22: Purl around to form a ridge.

Rnd 25: (K4, K2tog) around—165 sts.

Rnd 29: (K3, K2tog) around—132 sts.

Rnd 37: (K2, K2tog) around—99 sts.

Knit 3 more rnds.

BO all sts evenly. Fasten off.

MIDDLE PLEAT

With B and 24"-long circular needle, PU 99 sts in front loops of horizontal sts of BO edge on bottom pleat.

Knit 1 rnd, pm at beg of rnd.

Rnd 1: (K2, K1f&b) around—132 sts.

Knit all rnds even, except for the following rnds:

Rnd 5: (K3, K1f&b) around—165 sts.

Rnd 10: Purl around to form a ridge.

Rnd 13: (K3, K2tog) around—132 sts.

Rnd 19: (K2, K2tog) around—99 sts.

Rnd 27: (K1, K2tog) around—66 sts.

Change to 16"-long circular needle.

Knit 3 more rnds.

BO all sts evenly. Fasten off.

23 — PAGODA: PLEATED BERET

TOP PLEAT

With C and 16"-long circular needle, PU 66 sts in front loops of horizontal sts of BO edge on middle pleat.

Knit 1 rnd, pm at beg of rnd.

Rnd 1: (K2, K1f&b) around—88 sts.

Knit all rnds even except for the following rnds:

Rnd 5: (K3, K1f&b) around—110 sts.

Rnd 10: Purl around to form a ridge.

Rnd 13: (K4, K2tog) around to last 2 sts, K2—92 sts.

Rnd 17: (K3, K2tog) around to last 2 sts, K2—74 sts.

Rnd 21: (K2, K2tog) around to last 2 sts, K2—56 sts.

Change to dpns, 14 sts on each of 4 needles.

Rnd 25: (K1, K2tog) around to last 2 sts, K2—38 sts.

Rnd 29: K2tog around—19 sts.

Rnd 33: K2tog around to last st, K1—10 sts.

Knit 1 more rnd.

Fasten off, leaving end approx 10" long. Pull end through rem sts and tighten.

FINISHING

Weave in ends. Press pleats. Using tapestry needle and yarn, sew 1 st between each of the pleats to help keep the pleats flat. Use a hat pin to decorate and shape the beret.

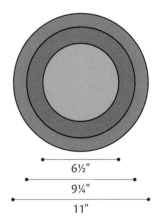

Top pleat →
Middle pleat →
Bottom pleat →
Band →

6½"
9¼"
11"

CONCERT: Concertina Bag

Shaped pleats create this little mystery of a bag. It flops when you put it down and opens up like an accordion when you hold it. I'm sure you haven't come across a bag like this before! Make it in a happy shade of Mango Moon's Elements or any non-stretch cordlike yarn like Great Adirondack Yarn Company's Elegance, and Judi & Company's Cordé.

Skill Level: Easy ◖■◻◻

Finished Measurements: Approx 12½" tall when extended, with a 9½"-diameter base

MATERIALS

4 skeins of Elements from Mango Moon (100% silk; 150 yards) in color 9502 Meadow (2 strands held tog throughout) 🎇5

US 10 (6 mm) circular needle (24" long)

Tapestry needle

Sewing needle and thread to match yarn

9½" x 9½" plastic sheet for base insert (an inexpensive plastic binder is a good source)

⅛" hole punch

GAUGE

12 sts and 24 rows = 4" in garter st with 2 strands held tog

BASE

The base is worked in garter st and has a seam.

Holding two strands of yarn tog, CO 119 sts.

Row 1: (K1, K2tog) to last 2 sts, K2—80 sts.

Rows 2–4: Knit.

Row 5: (K2, K2tog) to end—60 sts.

Rows 6–8: Knit.

Row 9: (K3, K2tog) to end—48 sts.

Rows 10–12: Knit.

Row 13: (K4, K2tog) to end—40 sts.

Rows 14–16: Knit.

Row 17: (K5, K2tog) to last 5 sts, K5—35 sts.

Rows 18–20: Knit.

Row 21: (K6, K2tog) to last 3 sts, K3—31 sts.

Rows 22–24: Knit.

Row 25: (K1, K2tog) to last st, K1—21 sts.

Row 26: K2tog to last st, K1—11 sts.

Pull yarn through rem sts, tighten, fasten off.

Sew the edges of the base tog to form a circle. Trace the base onto template plastic and cut out circle. Use a hole punch to make 9 holes evenly spaced around the circle about ⅛" from edge.

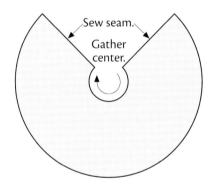

Sew seam.
Gather center.

PLEATED BODY

The body is worked back and forth in garter st and has a seam.

PU 117 sts around CO edge of base. Turn.

Rows 1–4: Knit.

Row 5 (dec): (K1, K2tog) to end—78 sts.

Rows 6–8: Knit.

Row 9 (dec): (K1, K2tog) to end—52 sts.

Rows 10–16: Knit.

Row 17 (inc): (K1, K1f&b) to end—78 sts.

Rows 18–20: Knit.

Row 21 (inc): (K1, K1f&b) to end—117 sts.

Rows 22–24: Knit.

Row 25: Purl to form a ridge.

Rep rows 2–25 once, and then rep rows 2–12 once.

BO all sts loosely.

FINISHING

Sew body seam. Weave in ends. Insert plastic base and sew to knitted base through holes with sewing needle and thread. There are 3 outside folds and 2 inside folds. Reinforce inside folds by stitching with a sewing needle close to the inside fold using running st and 1 strand of yarn. This will reinforce the center of the inside fold so that it doesn't pull out of shape.

Strap (Make 2.)

CO 3 sts.

Every row: Sl 1 pw, K2.

Work until strap is 23" long. BO. Weave in ends. Position straps symmetrically on opposite halves of bag. At 2" to the right of body seam, pull strap from outside to inside through a stitch close to the edge of the bag, and then pull strap through a stitch on both inside folds. Knot this end of strap. Strap length between each fold should be about 2", allowing bag to flop when put down and open up when held. Repeat for other end of first strap.

Position one end of second strap 2" left of seam. Attach as with first strap.

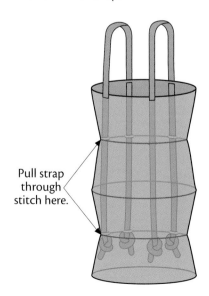

Pull strap through stitch here.

ACCORDION: Vertical Pleats Bag

A shaped base and vertically pleated front and back create a striking, roomy bag in versatile Lamb's Pride Bulky yarn.

Skill Level: Easy ◖■□□◗

Finished Measurements: Approx 12" tall and 18½" wide at base

MATERIALS

5 skeins of Lamb's Pride Bulky from Brown Sheep Company (85% wool/15% mohair; 113 g/4 oz; 125 yds/114 m) in color M186 Golden Mushroom ⑤

US 9 (5.5 mm) needles

18 stitch markers

Tapestry needle

Sewing needle and thread to match yarn

Pair of purchased handles

6" x 19" plastic sheet for base insert

⅛" hole punch

GAUGE

14 sts and 28 rows = 4" in garter st

BASE

CO 20 sts.

Rows 1 and 2: Sl 1 pw, knit to end.

Rows 3, 5, 7, 9, and 11: Sl 1 pw, K1f&b, knit to last 2 sts, K1f&b, K1—30 sts after row 11.

Rows 4, 6, 8, 10, and 12: Sl 1 pw, knit to end.

Rows 13 and 14: Sl 1 pw, knit to end.

Rows 15, 17, 19, 21, and 23: Sl 1 pw, K2tog, knit to last 3 sts, K2tog, K1—20 sts after row 23.

Rows 16, 18, 20, 22, and 24: Sl 1 pw, knit to end.

Work rows 1–24 another 4 times.

BO all sts.

Place finished knitted base on plastic sheet and trace around base. Cut out on drawn line.

FRONT AND BACK (MAKE 2.)

Sl 1 st at beg of every row.

Place markers as indicated in row 1 and slip them as you come to them in subsequent rows.

CO 103 sts.

Row 1: K15, *pm, K1, pm, K8, pm, sl 1 pw, pm, K8*, rep from * to * 3 times, pm, K1, pm, K15.

Row 2: Knit to marker, *sl 1 pw, knit to next marker, K1, knit to next marker*, rep from * to * 3 more times, sl 1 pw, knit to end.

Rep rows 1 and 2 for 2½".

Dec row: K1, K2tog, knit to next marker, *K1, knit to last 2 sts before next marker, K2tog, sl 1 pw, K2tog, knit to next marker*, rep from * to * 3 times, K1, knit to last 3 sts, K2tog, K1—93 sts.

Cont working rows 1 and 2 and AT SAME TIME work dec row every 2½" another 3 times—63 sts.

Work rows 1 and 2 for 1" after last dec row.

At beg of next 2 rows, BO 10 sts, cont in patt to end—43 sts.

Cont in established patt on rem sts and work 1 more dec row 2½" from last dec row as follows: K1, *K1, K2tog, K2, sl 1 pw, K2tog, K2, rep from * 3 times, K2—35 sts.

BO all sts on next RS row.

FINISHING

Sew front and back side seams tog. Use hole punch to make holes in plastic base evenly spaced around, about ⅛" from edges. Sew base to bottom of bag with sewing needle and thread. Sew handles at each end of top of bag.

GOLDEN FLEECE: Vicuña Collar

This is one very precious item of neckwear, no less luxurious and far softer on the skin than analogous adornments from the other Cartier. It is made of the rarest, most expensive natural fiber in the world—the mysterious vicuña. Cousin to llamas and alpacas, vicuñas were sacred to the Incas, and only Inca royalty were allowed to wear a full golden fleece. Spoil yourself as every true knitter should.

Qiviut and cashmere could also be used to make a luxurious collar. Try 100% Qiviut Fingering Weight from Nash Farms, or Mongolian Cashmere 2-ply from Jade Sapphire.

Skill Level: Intermediate ◖■■■◻

Size: One size to fit average woman's neck.

Finished Circumference: Approx 16"

MATERIALS
1 ball of 100% Vicuña by Jacques Cartier
(1 oz/28.5 g; 217 yds/198 m) ❷

US 2 (2.75 mm) needles

Spare US 0 (2 mm) needles to pick up stitches

2 removable stitch markers

Sewing needle and thread to match yarn

4 very small buttons or snaps (optional: pin or brooch)

GAUGE
8 sts and 9 rows = 1" in St st

FEATURED TECHNIQUES
"Full-Row Pleats in Stockinette Stitch" on page 9.

"Sectional Pleats in Stockinette Stitch" on page 9.

"Short Rows" on page 11.

COLLAR
The collar consists of left and right bow parts with shaped pleats. The parts are joined to the main collar, which features horizontal pleats of different depths.

Left Pleated Bow
CO 28 sts.

Work 12 rows in sl-st ribbing as follows: (Sl 1 pw, K1) across.

First (smaller) pleat
Change to St st with 3-st garter border at each end.

Row 1: Knit.

Row 2: K3, purl to last 3 sts, K3.

Work rows 1 and 2 throughout and AT SAME TIME work incs and decs.

Inc rows: Work incs on 7th and 13th rows as follows: Work 3 garter sts, M1, work in St st to last 3 sts, M1, work 3 garter sts—32 sts.

Dec rows: Work dec on 6th row and 12th row as follows: Work 3 garter sts, K2tog, work in St st to last 5 sts, ssk, work 3 garter sts—28 sts.

Make pleat (RS): Knit tog sts from left needle and all sts picked up from row 1, including garter-st borders.

Work short rows between first and second pleat as follows.

*Work 5 rows in established patt.

Short row: K14, turn, wrap last st worked, purl to end, turn, K13, knit tog next st and wrap, finish row.

Work 5 rows in established patt.*

Second (larger) pleat

Place removable markers in first and last sts on next row to mark beg of second pleat.

Cont in St st with 3-st garter borders and AT SAME TIME work incs and decs.

Inc rows: Work incs on 6th row and then every following 6th row 2 times as follows: Work 3 garter sts, M1, work in St to last 3 sts, M1, work 3 garter sts—34 sts.

Dec rows: Work decs on 6th row and then every following 6th row 2 times as follows: Work 3 garter sts, K2tog, work in St st to last 5 sts, ssk, work 3 garter sts—28 sts.

Make pleat (RS): Work as for first pleat, picking up sts on marked row of 2nd pleat.

Next WS row: Purl.

BO all sts.

Right Pleated Bow

Worked as for left pleated bow except for short rows (* to *). Instead, work short rows as follows:

Work 6 rows in St st in established patt.

Short row: K3, P11, turn, wrap last st worked, knit to end, turn, K3, P10, purl tog next st and wrap, finish row.

Work 4 rows in established patt.

Collar

Collar is worked from top to bottom and shaped with incs.

Make pleats across all sts.

CO 80 sts.

Top border: Work 6 rows in garter st.

Rows 1–6: Beg with knit row, work in St st. Place removable markers in first and last sts on row 2.

Row 7: Join pleat with sts picked up from row 2.

Rows 8–18: Work in St st. Place removable markers in first and last sts on row 12.

Row 19: Join pleat with sts picked up from row 12.

Row 20: Purl.

Row 21 (inc): K4, (M1, K8) to last 4 sts, K4—89 sts.

Rows 22–34: Work in St st. Place removable markers in first and last sts on row 26.

Row 35: Join pleat with sts picked up from row 26.

Row 36: Purl.

Row 37 (inc): K4, (M1, K9) to last 4 sts, K4—98 sts.

Rows 38–54: Work in St st. Place removable markers in first and last sts on row 44.

Row 55: Join pleat with sts picked up from row 44.

Row 56: Purl.

Row 57 (inc): K4, (M1, K10) to last 4 sts, K4—107 sts.

Row 58: Purl.

Bottom border: Work 6 rows in garter st.

BO all sts loosely.

Finishing

Sew left- and right-pleated bows to sides of collar. Steam lightly.

Sew 4 small buttons or snaps on ribbing of left pleated bow. Very small buttons do not require buttonholes; use sl sts in ribbing section of right pleated bow. If using snaps, sew half on WS of ribbing on right-pleated bow, and other half on RS of ribbing on left-pleated bow. You can also secure collar with a long pin or brooch.

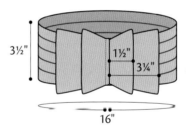

SILVER DARTS:
Sectional Pleats T-Shirt

Exceptionally pleasant to wear, this top will become a favorite for all seasons. Silk-and-wool fiber provides touchable softness; sectional pleats in the neck area and hips create an unusual accent.

Skill Level: Intermediate ■■■□

Sizes: Small (Medium, Large, Extra Large)

Finished Bust Measurement: 32 (33½, 35, 36¾)"

Finished Back Length: 25 (27, 29, 31)"

MATERIALS

8 (9, 10, 11) skeins of Synchronicity from Alchemy Yarns of Transformation (50% silk, 50% wool; 50 g/1.75 oz; 118 yds/108 m) in color 42m Silver ❨4❩

US 7 (4.5 mm) circular needle (24" long)

Spare US 4 (3.5 mm) needle to pick up stitches

1 stitch marker for beg of rnd

3 removable stitch markers

2 stitch holders

Size E-4 (3.5 mm) crochet hook

GAUGE

20 sts and 26 rows = 4" in St st

FEATURED TECHNIQUE

"Sectional Pleats in Stockinette Stitch" on page 9.

FRONT AND BACK

Top is worked in the rnd up to the armholes.

CO 160 (168, 176, 184) sts. Join and pm to indicate beg of rnd.

Rnds 1–11 (13, 15, 17): Work in St st.

Rnd 12 (14, 16, 18): [K40 (42, 44, 46), place removable marker] 3 times, K40 (42, 44, 46).

Rnds 13–24 (15–26, 17–28, 19–30): Work in St st.

Rnd 25 (27, 29, 31): K40 (42, 44, 46), *join pleat with 40 (42, 44, 46) sts picked up between markers on rnd 12 (14, 16, 18)*, K40 (42, 44, 46), rep join pleat from * to * on next 40 (42, 44, 46) sts. Remove markers.

Work rnd 2 through rnd 25 (27, 29, 31) another 2 times.

Work even for 7 (8, 9, 10)".

DIVIDE FOR FRONT AND BACK

K60 (63, 66, 69) sts and place on st holder for part of back, K80 (84, 88, 92) sts for front, place rem sts (20, 21, 22, 24) on a holder for rest of back. Pleats are now situated on sides of work.

FRONT

Work back and forth on 80 (84, 88, 92) sts in St st.

Purl 1 row.

Work armhole shaping as follows.

BO 5 sts at beg of next 2 rows—70 (74, 78, 82) sts.

Work decs at each end on every RS row 5 times as follows: K2tog, work to last 2 sts, ssk—60 (64, 68, 72) sts.

Rows 1–11 (13, 15, 17): Beg with knit row, work in St st.

Row 12 (14, 16, 18): P15 (17, 19, 21), place removable marker, P30, place removable marker, purl to end.

Rows 13–24 (15–26, 17–28, 19–30): Work in St st.

Row 25 (27, 29, 31): Join pleat on 30 sts between markers picked up from row 12 (14, 16, 18). Remove markers.

Rows 26–31 (28–35, 30–39, 32–43): Work in St st.

Work rows 12–31 (14–35, 16–39, 18–43) once more.

Work rows 12–25 (14–27, 16–29, 18–31) once.

Work 1 (3, 5, 7) row in St st.

BO all sts loosely.

BACK

Place sts from both holders onto needle. Work as for front.

CAP SLEEVES

Work dec as K2tog at beg of row and ssk at end of row.

CO 64 (70, 76, 82) sts.

Rows 1–9 (11, 13, 15): Beg with knit row, work in St st.

Row 10 (12, 14, 16) (WS): P17 (20, 23, 26), place removable marker, P30, place removable marker, purl to end.

Cont in St st and AT SAME TIME work cap shaping as follows.

BO 5 sts at beg of next 2 rows.

Dec 1 st at each end every 4 rows.

Rows 11–22 (13–24, 15–26, 17–28): Work in St st.

Row 23 (25, 27, 29): Join pleat on 30 sts between markers picked up on row 10 (12, 14, 16). Remove markers.

Rows 24–33 (26–35, 28–37, 30–39): Work in St st.

Row 34 (36, 38, 40): P13 (14, 19, 22), place removable marker, P20, place removable marker, purl to end.

Rows 35–46 (37–48, 39–50, 41–52): Work in St st.

Row 47 (49, 51, 53): Join pleat on 20 sts between markers picked up on row 34 (36, 38, 40). Remove markers.

Work 9 (11, 13, 15) rows in St st, maintaining dec every 4 rows.

BO 3 sts at beg of next 2 rows.

BO rem sts.

FINISHING

Sew 1½" of fronts to back for shoulders. Sew in sleeves. Sew sleeve seams tog. Weave in ends. With crochet hook, work 1 row of sc around sleeve and bottom edges. Steam or spray and leave to dry flat.

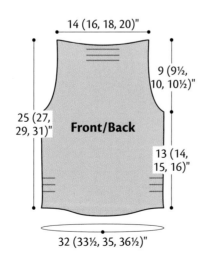

14 (16, 18, 20)"

9 (9½, 10, 10½)"

25 (27, 29, 31)"

Front/Back

13 (14, 15, 16)"

32 (33½, 35, 36½)"

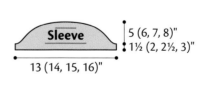

Sleeve

5 (6, 7, 8)"

1½ (2, 2½, 3)"

13 (14, 15, 16)"

RIBBONS AND TIES:
Sweet Pleated-Neck Bolero

This delightful little jacket in Be Sweet's innovative yarn is worked sideways and shaped with pleats along the neck edge. Ribbon ties on the yarn invite the use of additional ribbon as a finishing touch.

Skill Level: Intermediate ■■■□

Sizes: Small (Medium, Large)

Finished Bust Measurement: 42 (47, 52)"*

Finished Length: 16 (17, 18)"

*This is a very loose-fitting jacket and each measurement will fit a range of sizes.

MATERIALS

A 3 (4, 4) balls of African Bead Ball from Be Sweet Products (baby mohair with hand-tied glass beads; 50 g/1.75 oz; 120 yds/110 m) in color 18B Pale Green 🌀5

B 3 (4, 4) balls of Ribbon Ball from Be Sweet Products (baby mohair with hand-tied ribbons; 50 g/1.75 oz; 120 yds/110 m) in color 18B Pale Green 🌀5

US 11 (6.5 mm) circular needle (24" long)

Spare US 8 (5 mm) needle to pick up stitches

Size F-5 (3.75 mm) crochet hook

Approx 50 yds of ribbon, ⅛" (3 mm) wide

1 removable stitch marker

2 stitch holders

GAUGE

10 sts and 18 rows = 4" in St st

FEATURED TECHNIQUE

"Sectional Pleats in Stockinette Stitch" on page 9.

RIGHT FRONT

Work 2 rows in A, 2 rows in B throughout. Do not cut yarns, but carry them up the side, twisting at beg of every RS row.

With A, CO 40 (44, 48) sts.

Work 4 rows in garter st.

Change to St st.

Work 0 (2, 4) rows.

Rows 1 and 2: Beg with knit row, work St st.

Row 3 (inc): K1, M1, knit to end—41 (45, 49) sts.

Row 4: P20 (22, 24), place removable marker, purl to end.

Rows 5–8: Work in St st.

Row 9: Join pleat with sts picked up from row 4 to marker, remove marker, knit to end.

Row 10: Purl.

Row 11 (inc): K1, M1, knit to end—42 (46, 50) sts.

Row 12: P23 (25, 27), place removable marker, purl to end.

Rows 13–16: Work in St st.

Row 17: Join pleat with sts picked up from row 12 to marker, remove marker, knit to end.

Row 18: Purl.

Row 19 (inc): K1, M1, knit to end—43 (47, 51) sts.

Row 20: P26 (28, 30), place removable marker, purl to end.

Rows 21–24: Work in St st.

Row 25: Join pleat with sts picked up from row 20 to marker, remove marker, knit to end.

Row 26: Purl.

DIVIDE FOR LEFT ARMHOLE

Row 27: K1, M1, K22 (25, 27), cont on these 24 (27, 29) sts only, place rem sts on st holder for underarm.

Row 28: P10, place removable marker, purl to end.

Rows 29–32: Work in St st.

Row 33: Join pleat with sts picked up from row 28 to marker, knit to end.

Row 34: Purl.

Row 35 (inc): K1, M1, knit to end.

Row 36: P8, place removable marker, purl to end.

Rows 37–40: Work in St st.

Row 41: Join pleat with sts picked up from row 36 to marker, remove marker, knit to end.

Row 42: Purl.

Row 43: Knit.

Row 44: P10, place removable marker, purl to end.

Rep rows 29–44 twice, and then rep rows 29–35 once omitting incs.

Place sts on second st holder (do not cut yarn).

Place underarm sts on needle and join new ball of yarn.

Work 15 (17, 19) rows in St st, cut yarn.

BACK

Join armhole: With yarn attached to sts on first holder, knit across underarm sts on left needle—43 (47, 51) sts.

Start new row count.

Row 1: P30 (32, 34), place removable marker, purl to end.

Rows 2–5: Work in St st.

Row 6: Join pleat with sts picked up from row 1 to marker, remove marker, knit to end.

Row 7: Purl.

Row 8: Knit.

Row 9: P27 (29, 31), place removable marker, purl to end.

Rows 10–13: Work in St st.

Row 14: Join pleat with sts picked up from row 9 to marker, remove marker, knit to end.

Row 15: Purl.

Row 16: Knit.

Row 17: P30 (32, 34), place removable marker, purl to end.

For Small
Work rows 2–17 another 4 times.

For Medium
Work rows 2–17 another 5 times.

For Large
Work rows 2–17 another 6 times.

For all sizes
Work rows 2–7 once.

DIVIDE FOR RIGHT ARMHOLE

Next RS row: K1, M1, K22 (25, 27), cont on these 24 (27, 29) sts only, place rem sts on st holder for underarm.

Referring to "Divide for Left Armhole" and working K2tog instead of M1, work rows 36–44 once, rows 29–44 twice, and rows 29–43 once.

Place sts on 2nd st holder (do not cut yarn).

Place underarm sts on needle and join new ball of yarn.

Work 15 (17, 19) rows in St st, cut yarn.

Join armhole: With yarn attached to sts on first holder, knit across underarm sts on left needle—43 (47, 51) sts.

LEFT FRONT

Next WS row: P26 (28, 30), place removable marker, purl to end.

Start new row count.

Rows 1–4: Work in St st.

Row 5: Join pleat with sts picked up from first WS row in left front to marker, remove marker, knit to end.

Row 6: Purl.

Row 7 (dec): K1, K2tog, knit to end—42 (46, 50) sts.

Row 8: P23 (25, 27), place removable marker, purl to end.

Rows 9–12: Work in St st.

Row 13: Join pleat with sts picked up from row 8 to marker, remove marker, knit to end.

Row 14: Purl.

Row 15 (dec): K1, K2tog, knit to end—41 (45, 49) sts.

Row 16: P20 (22, 24), place removable marker, purl to end.

Rows 17–20: Work in St st.

Row 21: Join pleat with sts picked up from row 16 to marker, remove marker, knit to end.

Row 22: Purl.

Row 23 (dec): K1, K2tog, knit to end—40 (44, 48) sts.

Row 24: Purl.

Work 2 (4, 6) rows in St st.

Work 4 rows in garter st.

BO all sts loosely.

FINISHING

With ribbon and crochet hook, work 1 row of sc along bottom edge, armhole edges, and neck edge (do not stitch into pleats) as follows: Work 1 st into every row for bottom edge and armholes, and 1 st into every 2 rows on neck.

Cut 16 pieces of ribbon, each 1 yard long. Fold 8 pieces in half. From RS, insert folded ribbon into one side of jacket front, about 4" down from neck and 1" in from edge. Pull ends through fold and tighten. Attach remaining 8 lengths of ribbon to other side of front in same manner.

Steam bottom and armhole edges.

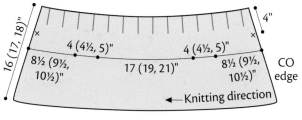

× Place ties.

WINGS: Butterfly Shawl

Inspired by the Japanese obi, this sculptural knit is both a conversation piece and a great cover-up for chilly shoulders. Basic stitches and shaped pleats take flight with wings.

Skill Level: Intermediate ■■■□

Finished Measurements: 11" x 60"

MATERIALS

3 skeins of Gossamer by Karabella (52% nylon, 30% kid mohair, 18% polyester; 50 g/1.78 oz; 222 yds/200 m) in color 6056 ▣③

US 8 (5 mm) needles

Spare US 6 (4.25 mm) needle to pick up stitches

US 10 (6 mm) needle for CO and BO

3 removable stitch markers

4 stitch holders

GAUGE

18 sts and 24 rows = 4" in St st

FEATURED TECHNIQUES

"Full-Row Pleats in Stockinette Stitch" on page 9.

"Puffy Pleats" on page 10.

LEFT END OF SHAWL

With size 10 needle, CO 50 sts.

Change to size 8 needle and work 4 rows in garter st.

Change to St st with 4-st garter border at each edge.

Row 1 (RS): Knit.

Row 2: K4, purl to last 4 sts, K4.

Rep rows 1 and 2 until piece measures 29", ending with a RS row.

Next WS row: K4, place removable marker, P24, place removable marker, P18, place removable marker, K4.

LEFT WINGS

Butterfly wings are wide, shaped horizontal pleats.

Left Bottom Wing

Row 1 (RS): K4 and place them on st holder, K18, place rem sts on st holder.

Bottom wing is worked on 18 sts with 3-st garter border at each edge.

Row 2: K3, P12, K3.

Rows 3 and 5: Knit.

Rows 4 and 6: K3, P12, K3.

Row 7 (inc): K3, M1, knit to end—19 sts.

Work in established patt and AT SAME TIME rep inc row on every 6th row 3 times—22 sts.

Work 6 rows in established patt.

Next row (dec): K3, K2tog, knit to end—21 sts.

Work in established patt and AT SAME TIME rep dec on every 6th row 3 times—18 sts.

Work 5 rows even.

Next RS row: Join pleat on 18 sts picked up from last WS row of left end of shawl. Place completed bottom wing sts on st holder.

Left Top Wing

Return 24 sts on holder to needle. Leave rem 4 sts on st holder.

Row 1: Knit.

Row 2: K3, purl to last 3 sts, K3.

Row 3 (inc): Knit to last 3 sts, M1, K3—25 sts.

Rep rows 1 and 2 and AT SAME TIME work inc row every 6th row 5 times—30 sts.

Work 5 rows even.

Next row (dec): Knit to last 5 sts, K2tog, K3—29 sts.

Cont as established and AT THE SAME TIME rep dec every 6th row 5 times—24 sts.

Work 1 WS row.

With WS facing you, and size 6 needle, pick up 24 sts between markers on last row of left end of shawl.

Next RS row: Join pleat on 24 sts picked up from last WS row of left end of shawl, knit across 4 border sts from holder.

Work 2 rows in St st with 4-st garter border at each end.

Next WS row: K4, place removable marker, purl to last 4 sts, place removable marker, K4.

BUTTERFLY BODY

A puffy pleat is worked for the body.

Row 1 (RS): K4 and put sts on st holder, K1f&b in each st to last 4 sts, turn and put rem 4 border sts on st holder.

Rows 2–9: Work in St st.

Row 10: P2tog across all sts of pleat, K4 from st holder.

Next row: K4, join pleat with sts picked up from last WS of left top wing, K4 from st holder.

Work 2 rows in St st.

Next WS row: K4, place removable marker, P24, place removable marker, P18, place removable marker, K4.

RIGHT WINGS

Work as for left wings except do not work last WS row of left top wing.

RIGHT END OF SHAWL

Work in St st with 4-st garter borders at each end until right end measures 29".

Work 4 rows in garter st.

BO loosely with size 10 needle.

FINISHING

Lightly steam edges. Butterfly wings can be stitched to main part of shawl to secure in place (as marked in diagram).

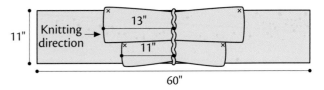

× Stitch to main piece.

VESTED INTEREST: Pleated-Back Vest

Simple horizontal pleats do most of the shaping
in this unusual vest. Knitting with the light, soft, beautifully
hand-dyed Malabrigo Twist is pure joy.

Skill Level: Intermediate ■■■□

Sizes: Small (Medium, Large, Extra Large)

Finished Bust Measurement: 36 (38, 40, 42)" after blocking

Finished Front Length: 21 (22½, 24, 25½)"

MATERIALS

4 (5, 5, 6) skeins of Twist from Malabrigo (100% pure baby merino wool; 100 g/3.5 oz; 150 yds/137 m) in color 618 Liquid Ambar ⑤

US 10 (6 mm) circular needle (36" long)

Spare US 7 (4.5 mm) needle to pick up stitches

2 stitch markers

2 removable stitch markers

2 stitch holders

Size F-5 (3.75 mm) crochet hook

GAUGE

14 sts and 22 rows = 4" in St st

FEATURED TECHNIQUE

"Sectional Pleats in Stockinette Stitch" on page 9.

BODY

Vest is worked in 1 piece up to armholes.

CO 124 (132, 140, 148) sts.

Rows 1–3: Beg with knit row, work in St st.

Row 4 (WS): P28, place removable marker, P68 (76, 84, 92), place removable marker, purl to end.

Rows 5–10: Work in St st.

Row 11: Join pleat with sts picked up between markers on row 4.

Rows 12 and 13: Work in St st.

Row 14: P18, place removable marker, P88 (96, 104, 112), place removable marker, purl to end.

Rows 15–20: Work in St st.

Row 21: Join pleat with sts picked up from row 14 between markers.

For Small: Rep rows 2–21 four times, and then rep rows 1–11 once.

For Medium: Rep rows 2–21 five times.

For Large: Rep rows 2–21 five times, and then rep rows 1–11 once.

For Extra Large: Rep rows 2–21 six times.

For all sizes, next WS row: P32 (34, 36, 38), pm, P60 (64, 68, 72), pm, P32 (34, 36, 38).

Divide for Fronts and Back

Knit to marker and remove it, put sts just worked on st holder for right front, knit to next marker (back) and remove it, put rem unworked sts on st holder for left front.

BACK

Pleats are worked across entire row.

Row 1: Purl.

Shape armholes

Rows 2 and 3: Work in St st, and BO 3 sts at beg of rows—54 (58, 62, 66) sts.

Rows 4 and 5: K2tog, work to last 2 sts, ssk—50 (54, 58, 62) sts. Place removable markers in first and last sts on row 5.

Rows 6–11: Work in St st.

Row 12: Join pleat across all sts, with sts picked up from row 5.

Rows 13–15: Work in St st. Place removable markers in first and last sts on row 15.

For Small: Rep rows 6–15 nine times.

For Medium: Rep rows 6–15 ten times.

For Large: Rep rows 6–15 eleven times.

For Extra Large: Rep rows 6–15 twelve times.

BO all sts.

RIGHT FRONT

Return right front sts to needle, purl 1 row.

Shape armhole: At armhole edge, work ssk at end of every RS row and P2tog at beg of every WS row until 1 st rem.

Fasten off.

LEFT FRONT

Return left front sts to needle, work 2 rows in St st.

Shape armhole: At armhole edge, work K2tog at beg of every RS row and P2tog at end of every WS until 1 st rem.

Fasten off.

FINISHING

Sew last BO st on fronts to edges of back. Work 1 row of sc, and then work 1 row of rev sc around front edges, back of neck, and armholes. Steam edges. Use a pin to fasten fronts.

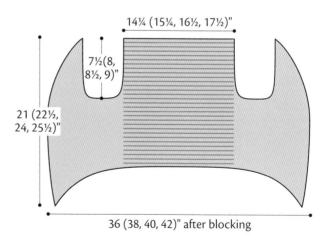

14¼ (15¼, 16½, 17½)"

7½(8, 8½, 9)"

21 (22½, 24, 25½)"

36 (38, 40, 42)" after blocking

FANNED: Three-Fan Shawl

My favorite Haiku yarn by Alchemy Yarns of Transformation turns this fan-shaped shawl into a truly special piece, an ethereal evocation of nature's patterns. Bobbles, pleats, and eyelets work together wonderfully to recall shells, butterflies, fossils, and flames.

Skill Level: Experienced ◗ ■ ■ ▶

Finished Measurements: Approx 17" x 58"

MATERIALS

3 skeins of Haiku from Alchemy Yarns of Transformation (60% mohair, 40% silk; 25 g/.88 oz; 325 yds/297 m) in color 76m Mother of Purl ⟨1⟩

US 10½ (6.5 mm) straight or circular needle (24" long)

US 7 (4.5 mm) straight or circular needle (24" long)

Spare US 4 (3.5 mm) needle to pick up stitches

Size B-1 (2.5 mm) crochet hook

2 removable stitch markers

GAUGE

20 sts and 22 rows = 4" in St st

FEATURED TECHNIQUES

"Full-Row Pleats in Stockinette Stitch" on page 9.

"Short Rows" on page 11.

"Reverse Stockinette Stitch Bobbles" on page 11.

SHAWL CENTER

With size 10½ needle, CO 70 sts.

Change to size 7 needle and purl 1 row.

Rows 1–8: Beg with knit row, work in St st. Place removable markers in first and last sts on row 1.

Row 9: Join pleat across all sts picked up from row 1.

Row 10: Purl.

Rows 11 and 12 (short row): K15, turn, wrap last st worked, purl to end.

Rows 13 and 14 (short row): K14, knit tog next st and wrap, K15, turn, wrap last st worked, purl to end.

Rows 15 and 16 (short row): K29, knit tog next st and wrap, K15, turn, wrap last st worked, purl to end.

Rows 17 and 18 (eyelet row/short row): K1, M1, K1, (YO, K2tog) 20 times, knit to wrapped st, knit tog next st and wrap, K15, turn, wrap last st worked, purl to end.

Rows 19 and 20 (short row): K45, turn, wrap last st worked, purl to end.

Rows 21 and 22 (short row): K30, turn, wrap last st worked, purl to end.

Rows 23 and 24 (short row): K15, turn, wrap last st worked, purl to end.

Row 25: Knit, working wraps and wrapped sts tog.

Row 26: Purl.

Rows 27–36: Rep rows 1–10.

Rows 37–42: Rep rows 11–16.

Rows 43 and 44 (bobble row/short row): K1, M1, K2, (MB, K5) 6 times, MB, knit to wrapped st, knit tog next st and wrap, K15, turn, wrap last st worked, purl to end.

Rows 45–52: Rep rows 19–26.

Rep rows 1–52 three times as given.

Rep rows 1–52 four times *working K2tog in place of M1.*

Rep rows 1–36 once *working K2tog in place of M1.*

BO all sts with size 10½ needle.

SIDES (MAKE 2.)

With size 10½ needle, CO 45 sts.

Change to size 7 needles and purl 1 row.

Rows 1–8: Beg with knit row, work in St st. Place removable markers in first and last sts on row 1.

Row 9: Join pleat across all sts picked up from row 1.

Row 10: Purl.

Rows 11 and 12 (short row): K10, turn, wrap last st worked, purl to end.

Rows 13 and 14 (short row): K9, knit tog next st and wrap, K10, turn, wrap last st worked, purl to end.

Rows 15 and 16 (short row): K19, knit tog next st and wrap, K10, turn, wrap last st worked, purl to end.

Rows 17 and 18 (eyelet row/short row): K1, M1, K1, (YO, K2tog) 12 times, knit to wrapped st, knit tog next st and wrap, K10, turn, wrap last st worked, purl to end.

Rows 19 and 20 (short row): K30, turn, wrap last st worked, purl to end.

Rows 21 and 22 (short row): K20, turn, wrap last st worked, purl to end.

Rows 23 and 24 (short row): K10, turn, wrap last st worked, purl to end.

Row 25: Knit, working wraps and wrapped sts tog.

Row 26: Purl.

Rows 27–36: Rep rows 1–10.

Rows 37–42: Rep rows 11–16.

Rows 43 and 44 (bobble row/short row): K1, M1, K2, (MB, K5) 4 times, MB, knit to wrapped st, knit tog next st and wrap, K10, turn, wrap last st worked, purl to end.

Rows 45–52: Rep rows 19–26.

Rep rows 1–52 once as given.

Rep rows 1–52 twice *working K2tog in place of M1.*

Rep rows 1–36 once *working K2tog in place of M1.*

BO all sts with size 10½ needle.

FINISHING

Sew smaller side pieces to center piece. Thread tapestry needle with 4 strands of yarn. Leaving a long tail, weave yarn in and out along base of each fan, leaving a long tail at opposite end. Pull ends tog to gather the base, and then tie a knot and weave ends into inside of nearest pleat. Using crochet hook and 2 strands of yarn held tog, work 1 row of sc, and then 1 row of rev sc all around the shawl. At each gathered base, sc into the spaces between gathered pleats, not the actual pleats. Steam edges gently.

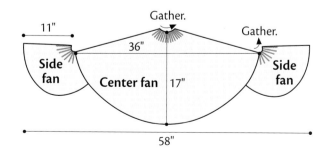

BORDERLINES: Pleated-Trim Jacket

This close-fitting jacket looks classic despite the unusual sideways knitting of the body and interesting shaping on the hips. Use a striking button or pin, or wear it unfastened. The pleated borders serve as a stand-up collar.

Skill Level: Intermediate ■■■□

Sizes: Small (Medium, Large, Extra Large)

Finished Bust Measurement: 34 (38, 42, 46)"

Finished Back Length: 25 (26, 27, 28½)"

MATERIALS

10 (12, 14, 16) skeins of Worsted Hand Dyes from Blue Sky Alpacas (50% royal alpaca, 50% merino; 100 g; 100 yds/91 m) in color 2003 (4)

US 10½ (6.5 mm) circular needle (36" long)

Spare US 8 (5 mm) circular needle (24" long) to pick up stitches

Size F-5 (3.75 mm) crochet hook

3 stitch markers

2 removable stitch markers

1 large decorative button or pin, approx 1¾" to 2" diameter or length

GAUGE

14 sts and 21 rows = 4" in St st

FEATURED TECHNIQUE

"Full-Row Pleats in Stockinette Stitch" on page 9.

FRONT AND BACK (MAKE 2.)

CO 176 (184, 192, 200) sts.

Rows 1–9: Beg with purl row, work in St st. Place removable markers in first and last sts on row 5.

Row 10: Join pleat with sts picked up from row 5.

Rows 11–21: Work in St st. Place removable markers in first and last sts on row 17.

Row 22: Join pleat with sts picked up from row 17.

Work rows 11–22 another 3 times (5 pleats made).

Row 55: P24 (26, 28, 30), pm, P64 (66, 68, 70), pm, P64 (66, 68, 70), pm, P24 (26, 28, 30).

Shape Hips and Shoulders

Row 56 (dec row): Knit to marker, K2tog, knit to last 2 sts before marker, ssk, knit to last 2 sts before next marker, ssk, knit to end.

Row 57: Purl, maintaining markers.

Row 58: Knit.

Row 59: Purl.

Row 60 (dec row): Knit to marker, ssk, knit to marker, K2tog, knit to last 2 sts before next marker, K2tog, knit to end.

Row 61: Purl.

Row 62: Knit.

Row 63: Purl.

For Small
Rep rows 56–63 once—164 sts.

For Medium
Rep rows 56–63 once and rows 56–59 once—169 sts.

For Large
Rep rows 56–63 twice—174 sts.

For Extra Large
Rep rows 56–63 twice and rows 56–59 once—179 sts.

For All Sizes

Next RS row: K63 (64, 66, 67), BO center 38 (41, 42, 45) sts, place right-side sts on spare needle and cont on left side only, K63 (64, 66, 67).

Left Side

Row 1: Purl.

Row 2: Ssk, knit to last 2 sts before marker, K2tog, knit to end.

Row 3: Purl.

Row 4: Ssk, knit to end.

Row 5: Purl.

Row 6: Ssk, knit to 2 sts before marker, ssk, knit to end.

Row 7: Purl.

Row 8: Ssk, knit to end.

For Small: No rep—57 sts.

For Medium: Rep rows 1–4 once—55 sts.

For Large: Rep rows 1–8 once—54 sts.

For Extra Large: Rep rows 1–8 once and rows 1–4 once—52 sts.

For All Sizes

Next WS row: BO 24 (26, 28, 30) sts pw, purl to end.

Next RS row: Ssk, knit to end.

Next WS row: BO 15 sts pw, purl to end.

Next RS row: Knit.

BO rem 17 (13, 10, 6) sts pw.

Right Side

Rejoin yarn to sts on spare needle at armhole edge ready to work a purl row.

Row 1: Purl.

Row 2: Knit to marker, ssk, knit to last 2 sts, K2tog.

Row 3: Purl.

Row 4: Knit to last 2 sts, K2tog.

Row 5: Purl.

Row 6: Knit to marker, K2tog, knit to last 2 sts, K2tog.

Row 7: Purl.

Row 8: Knit to last 2 sts, K2tog.

For Small: No rep—57 sts.

For Medium: Rep rows 1–4 once—55 sts.

For Large: Rep rows 1–8 once—54 sts.

For Extra Large: Rep rows 1–8 once and 1–4 once—52 sts.

For All Sizes

Next WS row: Purl.

Next RS row: BO 24 (26, 28, 30) sts, knit to last 2 sts, K2tog.

Next WS row: Purl.

Next RS row: BO 15 sts, knit to end.

Next WS row: Purl.

BO rem 17 (13, 10, 6) sts.

SLEEVES

CO 38 (42, 46, 50) sts.

Rows 1–9: Beg with purl row, work in St st. Place removable markers in first and last sts on row 5.

Row 10: Join pleat with sts picked up from row 5.

Rows 11–21: Work in St st. Place removable markers in first and last sts on row 17.

Row 22: Join pleat with sts picked up from row 17.

Work rows 11–22 another 3 times (5 pleats made).

Sleeve incs: Cont in St st, and work incs every 10 rows 8 (8, 9, 9) times as follows: work 1 st, M1, work to last st, M1, work last st—54 (58, 64, 68) sts.

Work even until piece measures 16 (17, 18, 19)".

Shape cap:

BO 4 sts at beg of next 2 rows.

BO 2 sts at beg of next 2 rows.

Work decs at each side on every RS row 10 (12, 14, 16) times as follows: K2tog at beg of row and ssk at end of row.

BO 3 sts at beg of next 2 rows.

BO rem (16, 16, 18, 18) sts.

FINISHING

Sew sleeves into armholes. Sew sleeve seams and side seams. Sew front and back pieces tog making a seam in the middle of the back, starting about 3" from shoulder line and sewing to about 4" from bottom edge. Or for wider hips, you can leave the bottom open up to the hip dec line. Weave in all ends.

Steam all seams and pleated parts lightly.

Sew button close to the edge at desired place (about 12" from bottom edge in the original). Mark corresponding spot on the right front. To crochet a loop buttonhole, attach small length of yarn (approx 12" long) to WS of the right front about 1" in from the edge and 1" above the button. Ch 14, attach yarn 1" below start of chain, fasten off, and weave in ends.

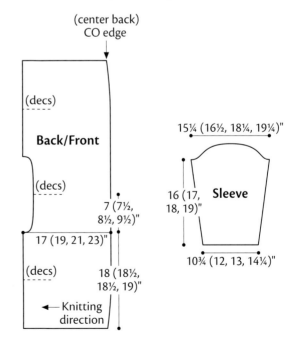

EVE'S RIBS:
Horizontal Ribbed Pullover

This unusual pullover drapes beautifully due to the pleated ribbing pattern, shaped waistline, and wonderful quality of the yarn.

Skill Level: Intermediate ◧◧◧▢

Size: To fit Small to Medium

Finished Bust Measurement: 34" to 36"; very stretchy

Finished Back Length: 24"

MATERIALS

5 skeins of Silk Rhapsody from Art Yarns (80% silk, 20% mohair; 100 g/3.5 oz; 260 yds/238 m) in color 114 ④

US 7 (4.5 mm) circular needles (16" and 36" long)

Spare US 4 (3.5 mm) needle to pick up stitches

2 stitch markers in different colors

4 removable stitch markers

GAUGE

19 sts and 24 rows = 4" in horizontal ribbing

FEATURED TECHNIQUES

"Sectional Pleats in Horizontal Ribbing" on page 10.

"Short Rows" on page 11.

FRONT AND BACK

Front and back are worked in the rnd up to the armholes.

CO 160 sts. Join to work in rnds.

Rnds 1–5: Knit, placing first st marker at beg of rnd 1, K80, place second st marker to indicate half of sweater.

Rnd 6: *K31, place removable marker, K18, place removable marker, K31*; rep from * to *.

Rnds 7–12: Purl.

Rnd 13: *K31, join pleat on 18 sts picked up between markers, K31*; rep from * to *.

Rnds 14–17: Knit.

Rnd 18: *K29, place removable marker, K22, place removable marker, K29*; rep from * to *.

Rnds 19–24: Purl.

Rnd 25: *K29, join pleat on 22 sts picked up between markers, K29*; rep from * to *.

Rnds 26–29: Knit.

Rnd 30: *K31, place removable marker, K18, place removable marker, K31*; rep from * to *.

Rnds 31–36: Purl.

Rnd 37: *K31, join pleat on 18 sts picked up between markers, K31*; rep from * to *.

Rnds 38 and 39: Knit.

Rnd 40 (first dec rnd): K1, K2tog, knit to last 3 sts before 2nd marker, ssk, K1, sm, K1, K2tog, knit to last 3 sts before beg-of-rnd marker, ssk, K1—156 sts.

Rnd 41: Knit.

Rnd 42: *K28, place removable marker, K22, place removable marker, K28*; rep from * to *.

Rnd 43–48: Purl.

Rnd 49: *K28, join pleat on 22 sts picked up between markers, K28*; rep from * to *.

Rnds 50 and 51: Knit.

Rnd 52 (second dec rnd): Work as rnd 40—152 sts.

Rnd 53: Knit.

Rnd 54: *K29, place removable marker, K18, place removable marker, K29*; rep from * to *.

Rnds 55–60: Purl.

Rnd 61: *K29, make pleat on 18 sts picked up between markers, K29*; rep from * to *.

Rnds 62 and 63: Knit.

Rnd 64 (third dec rnd): Work as rnd 40—148 sts.

Rnd 65: Knit and reposition st markers as follows: K37, place st marker to indicate new beg of rnd, K74 (removing old marker), pm after 74th st to indicate new half of sweater.

Rnd 66: *K26, place removable marker, K22, place removable marker, K26*, sm; rep from * to *.

Rnds 67–72: Purl.

Rnd 73: *K26, join pleat on 22 sts picked up between markers, K26*; rep from * to *.

Rnds 74–77: Knit.

Rnd 78: *K28, place removable marker, K18, place removable marker, K28*; rep from * to *.

Rnds 79–84: Purl.

Rnd 85: *K28, join pleat on 18 sts picked up between markers, K28*; rep from * to *.

Rnds 86–89: Knit.

Rnd 90: *K26, place removable marker, K22, place removable marker, K26*, sm; rep from * to *.

Rnds 91–96: Purl.

Rnd 97: *K26, join pleat on 22 sts picked up between markers, K26*; rep from * to *.

Rnds 98 and 99: Knit.

Rnd 100 (inc rnd): *K36, M1, K2, M1, K36*, sm; rep from* to *—152 sts.

Rnd 101: Knit.

Rnd 102: *K29, place removable marker, K18, place removable marker, K29*, sm; rep from * to *.

Rnds 103–108: Purl.

Rnd 109: *K29, join pleat on 18 sts picked up between markers, K29*, sm; rep from * to *.

Rnds 110 and 111: Knit.

Rnd 112 (inc rnd): *K37, M1, K2, M1, K37*, sm; rep from * to *—156 sts.

Rnd 113: Knit.

Rnd 114: *K28, place removable marker, K22, place removable marker, K28*, sm; rep from * to *.

Rnds 115–120: Purl.

Rnd 121: *K28, join pleat on 22 sts picked up between markers, K28*; rep from * to *.

Rnd 122: Move st markers to their original position at the sides as follows: K39, place first st marker for beg of rnd, K78, place second st marker, K39.

Rnds 123–125: Knit.

Rnd 126: *K29, place removable marker, K18, place removable marker, K29*, sm; rep from * to *.

FRONT

Divide for front and back

Row 1 (RS): BO 4 sts, purl to second marker, turn, remove marker, put rem 78 sts on holder for back. Cont on front 74 sts.

Row 2: BO 4 sts, knit to end—70 sts.

Row 3: BO 2 sts, purl to end—68 sts.

Row 4: BO 2 sts, knit to end—66 sts.

Row 5 (dec row): P2tog, purl to last 2 sts, P2tog—64 sts.

Row 6: Knit.

Row 7 (dec row): K2tog, K22, join pleat on 18 sts picked up between markers, K22, K2tog—62 sts.

Rows 8 and 10: Purl.

Rows 9 and 11 (dec rows): K2tog, knit to last 2 sts, K2tog—58 sts.

Row 12: P18, place removable marker, P22, place removable marker, P18.

Rows 13–18: Work in rev St st.

Row 19: K18, join pleat on 22 sts picked up between markers, K18.

Rows 20–23: Work in St st.

Row 24: P20, place removable marker, P18, place removable marker, P20.

Rows 25–30: Work in rev St st.

Row 31: K20, join pleat on 18 sts picked up between markers, K20.

Rows 32–35: Work in St st.

Row 36: P18, place removable marker, P22, place removable marker, P18.

Rows 37–42: Work in rev St st.

Rows 43–60: Rep rows 19-36 without placing markers on row 36.

BO all sts loosely.

BACK

Place sts on holder back on needle, rejoin yarn to sts.

Row 1: BO 4 sts, purl to end.

Rows 2–60: Work as for front.

SLEEVES

Sleeves are worked sideways in horizontal ribbing, shaped with incs and decs at top edge and short rows. There are no pleats made on sleeves.

CO 64 sts.

Row 1 (RS): Knit.

Row 2: Purl.

Rows 3 and 4: Knit to last 15 sts, turn, sl next st as if to purl wyib, purl to end.

Row 5: Knit.

Row 6: Purl.

Work rows 7–18 as follows and AT SAME TIME M1 at right-hand edge of every row.

Rows 7–12: Work in rev St st.

Row 13: Knit.

Row 14: Purl.

Rows 15 and 16: Knit to last 30 sts, turn, sl next st as if to purl wyib, purl to end.

Row 17: Knit.

Row 18: Purl—76 sts.

Rows 19–24: Work as rows 7–12, M1 between first and second st at beg of every RS row—79 sts.

Rows 25–30: Work as rows 1–6, M1 between first and second st at beg of every RS row—82 sts.

Rows 31–36: Work as rows 7–12, M1 between first and second st at beg of every RS row—85 sts.

Rows 37–42: Work as rows 1–6, M1 between first and second st at beg of row 39—86 sts.

Rows 43–48: Work as rows 7–12, M1 between first and second st at beg of row 43—87 sts.

Rows 49–54: Work in St st.

Rows 55–60: Work in rev St st, K2tog at beg of row 59—86 sts.

Rows 61–66: Work as rows 1–6, K2tog at beg of row 63—85 sts.

Rows 67–72: Work in rev St st, K2tog at beg of every RS row—82 sts.

Rows 73–78: Work as rows 1–6, K2tog at beg of every RS row—79 sts.

Rows 79–84: Work in rev St st, K2tog at beg of every RS row—76 sts.

Work rows 85–96 as follows and AT SAME TIME at right-hand edge K2tog on every RS row and P2tog on every WS row.

Row 85: Knit.

Row 86: Purl.

Rows 87 and 88: Knit to last 30 sts, turn, sl next st as if to purl wyib, purl to end.

Row 89: Knit.

Row 90: Purl.

Rows 91–96: Work in rev St st—64 sts.

Row 97: Knit.

Row 98: Purl.

Rows 99 and 100: Knit to last 15 sts, turn, sl next st as if to purl wyib, purl to end.

Row 101: Knit.

Row 102: Purl.

BO all sts.

FINISHING

Sew 1½" of front and back BO edges tog for shoulders. Sew in sleeves. Sew sleeve seams. Blocking is not recommended for Silk Rhapsody because of its texture.

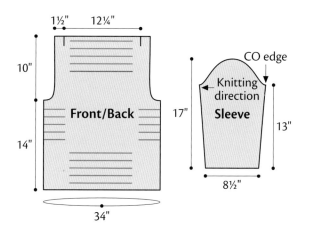

LONG WAY BACK:
Elongated-Back Pullover

Horizontal pleats accentuate the unusual shape of
this pullover, with its elongated back that elegantly provides a bit of
extra coverage—perfect for cold-weather outings.

Skill Level: Intermediate ◼◼◼▢

Sizes: Small (Medium, Large, Extra Large)

Finished Bust Measurement: 38 (40, 42½, 45)"

Finished Back Length: 26 (26½, 27, 27½)"

MATERIALS

6 (7, 8, 9) skeins of Groovy from Dream in Color (100% superfine Australian merino; 4 oz; 120 yds) in color VF03S Grey Tabby ⑤

US 10½ (6.5 mm) circular needles (16", 24", and 36" long)

Spare US 8 (5 mm) needle to pick up stitches

3 stitch markers (1 a different color for beg of rnd)

2 removable stitch markers

1 stitch holder

GAUGE

12 sts and 18 rows = 4" in St st

FEATURED TECHNIQUE

"Sectional Pleats in Horizontal Ribbing" on page 10.

FRONT AND BACK BORDER

Border is worked in the rnd and shaped with decs in middle of back.

Using 36"-long circular needle, CO 142 (150, 158, 166) sts. Place left side marker, join to work in the rnd.

Rnds 1–3: Knit.

Rnd 4: K15 (17, 19, 21), place removable pleat marker, K30, place removable pleat marker, K15 (17, 19, 21), place right side st marker, K41 (43, 45, 47), place middle of back st marker, K41 (43, 45, 47).

Rnds 5–8: Purl.

Rnd 9: K15 (17, 19, 21), join pleat on 30 sts picked up between pleat markers, K15 (17, 19, 21), sm, knit to last 2 sts before next st marker K2tog, sm, K2tog, knit to end—140 (148, 156, 164) sts.

Maintain side and middle of back st markers in place, as number of sts between them changes.

Rnds 10 and 11: Knit.

Row 12: K15 (17, 19, 21), place removable pleat marker, K30, place removable pleat marker, knit to end.

Work rnds 5–12 another 3 times, and then work rnds 5–8 once—134 (142, 150, 158) sts.

Divide for Front and Back

With 24"-long needle, K15 (17, 19, 21), join pleat on 30 sts picked up between markers, K15 (17, 19, 21). Remove side st markers. Turn and work front back and forth in St st. Place rem 74 (78, 82, 86) sts for back on st holder.

FRONT

Work 9 (11, 13, 15) rows in St st.

Shape armholes: BO 4 sts at beg of next 2 rows. BO 2 sts at beg of next 2 rows. Dec 1 st at both sides on every RS row 3 times—42 (46, 50, 54) sts.

Work in St st until length from top of border measures 6½ (7, 7½, 8)".

Shape left neck and shoulders: K12 (13, 14, 15), turn and work left shoulder. Dec 1 st 3 times on every RS row at neck edge—9 (10, 11, 12) sts.

Work until armhole measures 8½ (9½, 10½, 11½)". BO rem sts.

Shape right neck and shoulders: Rejoin yarn, BO 18 (20, 22, 24) center sts, K12 (13, 14, 15). Work in St st, and dec 1 st 3 times on every RS row at neck edge—9 (10, 11, 12) sts.

Cont in St st until right shoulder is same length as left shoulder. BO rem sts.

BACK

Lower back is worked in short rows.

Transfer sts onto 24"-long circular needle so you have left half of back plus 5 sts of the right half on left needle and rem sts of right half of the back on your right needle. Rejoin yarn at this division point.

Row 1: With right-hand needle, K10 center sts, removing marker at middle of back.

Row 2: Turn, wrap, P11.

Row 3: Turn, wrap, K10, knit tog wrap and wrapped st, K1.

Row 4: Turn, wrap, P11, purl tog wrap and wrapped st, P1.

Row 5: Turn, wrap, K12, knit tog wrap and wrapped st, K1.

Cont in this manner, working to wrapped st, knitting tog wrap and wrapped st, and then working 1 more st before turning, until all sts are used up and there are 74 (78, 82, 86) sts on 1 needle.

Work 10 (12, 14, 16) rows in St st and AT SAME TIME dec 1 st on every row at each end 7 times—60 (64, 68, 72) sts.

Shape armholes: Work as for front—42 (46, 50, 54) sts. Work even until armhole measures 6½ (7, 7½, 8)".

Shape left neck and shoulders: K10 (11, 12, 13), turn and finish left shoulder. Dec 1 st at neck edge on next RS row—9 (10, 11, 12) sts. Work even until armhole measures 8½ (9½, 10½, 11½)". BO all sts.

Shape right neck and shoulders: Rejoin yarn to rem sts, BO center 20 (22, 24, 26) sts, K10 (11, 12, 13). Dec 1 st at neck edge on next RS row—9 (10, 11, 12) sts. Work even until length matches left shoulder. BO all sts.

SLEEVES

CO 32 (34, 36, 38) sts.

Row 1: Purl.

Row 2: Knit.

Row 3: P8 (9, 10, 11), place removable marker, P16, place removable marker, P8 (9, 10, 11).

Rows 4–7: Work in rev St st.

Row 8: K8 (9, 10, 11), join pleat on 16 sts picked up between markers in row 3, K8 (9, 10, 11).

Work rows 1–8 another 4 times.

Change to St st and M1 at each side every 10 rows 5 (5, 6, 6) times. When sleeve measures 16 (17, 18, 19)", shape cap.

Shape cap: BO 4 sts at beg of next 2 rows. BO 2 sts at beg of next 2 rows. Dec 1 st at each end on every RS row 9 (10, 11, 12) times.

BO rem 12 (12, 14, 14) sts.

COLLAR

Sew tog shoulder seams. With 16"-long circular needle, beg at right shoulder seam, PU 34 (36, 38, 40) sts from back of neck opening and 44 (46, 48, 50) sts from front neck opening, pm to indicate beg of rnd.

Rnds 1 and 2: Knit.

Rnd 3: K34 (36, 38, 40), K13 (14, 15, 16), place removable marker, K18, place removable marker, K13 (14, 15, 16).

Rnds 4–7: Purl.

Rnd 8: K34 (36, 38, 40), K13 (14, 15, 16), join pleat on 18 sts picked up between markers in row 3, K13 (14, 15, 16).

Work rnds 1–8 another 4 times.

Using larger needle, BO all sts loosely.

FINISHING

Set in sleeves and sew sleeve seams tog. Sew tog side seams above border. Weave in ends. Steam and stretch CO edge of the border.

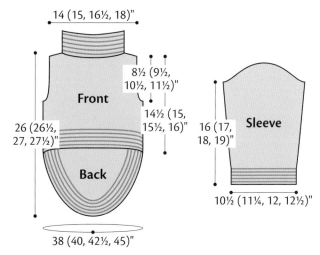

14 (15, 16½, 18)"

Front

8½ (9½, 10½, 11½)"

14½ (15, 15½, 16)"

26 (26½, 27, 27½)"

Back

38 (40, 42½, 45)"

Sleeve

16 (17, 18, 19)"

10½ (11¼, 12, 12½)"

LIPSTICK GLAMOUR:
Top with Vertical Pleats

The combination of two unusual yarns makes pleating
easier and gives this top a great texture. And what a fantastic
neckline—put on your lipstick and go party!

Skill Level: Intermediate ■■■□

Sizes: Small (Medium)

Finished Bust Measurement: 34 (38)"

Finished Length: 19½ (21½)"

MATERIALS

A 6 (7) skeins of Angora from Prism Yarns (100% French angora; 1 oz; 90 yds) in color Lipstick ⑤

B 5 (6) skeins of Tulle from Prism Yarns (100% nylon; 1 oz; 96 yds) in color Lipstick

US 7 (4.5 mm) needles ⑤

Spare US 4 (3.5 mm) needle to pick up stitches

1 removable stitch marker

GAUGE

14 sts and 22 rows = 4" in St st

FEATURED TECHNIQUE

"Sectional Pleats in Stockinette Stitch" on page 9.

BACK

Top worked sideways in St st with partial pleats of different length throughout.

For Medium, extra width is provided in the beginning, the shoulders, and the neck shaping.

Pleat rows are worked in A, and gap rows are worked in B.

Do not cut yarns when changing yarns. Carry them up the side, twisting at beg of every RS row.

Left Armhole and Shoulder Section

With larger needle and B, CO 45 (50) sts and work 0 (4) rows in St st.

Rows 1–5: Beg with knit row and B, work in St st.

Row 6: P25, place removable stitch marker, purl to end.

Rows 7–12: Change to A, work in St st.

Row 13: Change to B, join pleat with sts picked up to marker, remove marker, knit to end.

Rows 14 and 16: Purl.

Rows 15 and 17: K1, M1, knit to end.

Row 18: P15, place removable marker, purl to end.

Rows 19–24: Change to A, work in St st.

Row 25: Change to B, join pleat with sts picked up to marker, remove marker, knit to end.

Rows 26 and 28: Purl.

Row 27: CO 3 sts, knit to end.

Row 29: CO 20 (22) sts, knit to end.

Row 30: P25, place removable marker, purl to end.

Rows 31–36: Change to A, work in St st.

Row 37: Change to B, join pleat with sts picked up to marker, remove marker, knit to end.

Rows 38 and 40: Purl.

Row 39: K1, M1, knit to end.

Row 41: Knit.

Row 42: P15, place removable marker, purl to end.

Rows 43–48: Change to A, work in St st.

Rows 49–53: Rep rows 37–41.

Row 54: P25, place removable marker, purl to end.

For Small
Rep rows 31–36.

For Medium
Rep rows 37–48.

For Both Sizes

Next RS row: Change to B, join pleat with sts picked up to marker, remove marker, knit to end.

Next WS row: Purl.

NECK SHAPING DECREASES

Start new row count.

Row 1: Cont with B, BO 3 sts, knit to end.

Row 2: Purl.

Row 3: BO 2 sts, knit to end.

Small Row 4: P15, place removable marker, purl to end.

Medium Row 4: P25, place removable marker, purl to end.

Rows 5–10: Change to A, work in St st.

Row 11: Change to B, join pleat with sts picked up to marker, remove marker, knit to end.

Rows 12 and 14: Purl.

Row 13: K2tog, knit to end.

Row 15: Knit.

Small Row 16: P25, place removable marker, purl to end.

Medium Row 16: P15, place removable marker, purl to end.

Rows 17–22: Change to A, work in St st.

Row 23: Change to B, join pleat with sts picked up to marker, remove marker, knit to end.

Rows 24–27: Work in St st.

Row 28: As row 4 for Small and Medium.

Rows 29–34: Change to A, work in St st.

Row 35: Change to B, join pleat with sts picked up to marker, remove marker, knit to end.

Rows 36–39: Work in St st.

Row 40: As row 16 for Small and Medium.

For Small
Rep rows 17–22.

For Medium
Rep rows 17–34 as given.

NECK SHAPING INCREASES

Start new row count.

Row 1: Change to B, join pleat with sts picked up to marker, remove marker, knit to end.

Rows 2 and 4: Purl.

Row 3: K1, M1, knit to end.

Row 5: Knit.

Row 6: P15, place removable marker, purl to end.

Rows 7–12: Change to A, work in St st.

Row 13: Change to B, join pleat with sts picked up to marker, remove marker, knit to end.

Rows 14 and 16: Purl.

Row 15: CO 2 sts, knit to end.

Row 17: CO 3 sts, knit to end.

Row 18: P25, place removable marker, purl to end.

Last 2 rows beg the right shoulder.

RIGHT SHOULDER AND ARMHOLE

Rows 1–6: Change to A, work in St st.

Row 7: Change to B, join pleat with sts picked up to marker, remove marker, knit to end.

Rows 8 and 10: Purl.

Rows 9 and 11: Knit.

Row 12: P15, place removable marker, purl to end.

Rows 13–18: Change to A, work in St st.

Row 19: Change to B, join pleat with sts picked up to marker, remove marker, knit to end.

Rows 20 and 22: Purl.

Row 21: K2tog, knit to end.

Row 23: Knit.

Row 24: P25, place removable marker, purl to end.

Rows 25–30: Change to A, work in St st.

For Small
No repeats.

For Medium
Rep rows 19–23.

Next row: P15, place removable marker, purl to end.

Rep rows 25–30.

For Both Sizes

Row 31: As row 19.

Row 32: Purl.

Row 33: BO 20 (22) sts, knit to end.

Row 34: Purl.

Row 35: BO 3 sts, knit to end.

Small Row 36: P15, place removable marker, purl to end.

Medium Row 36: P25, place removable marker, purl to end.

Rows 37–42: Change to A, work in St st.

Row 43: Change to B, join pleat with sts picked up to marker, remove marker, knit to end.

Rows 44 and 46: Purl.

Rows 45 and 47: K2tog, knit to end.

Small Row 48: P25, place removable marker, purl to end.

Medium Row 48: P15, place removable marker, purl to end.

Rows 49–54: Change to A, work in St st.

Row 55: Change to B, join pleat with sts picked up to marker, remove marker, knit to end.

Work 5 rows in St st.

BO all sts.

FRONT

Work as for back, except for the following rows in the neck shaping decreases.

Row 1 in neck-shaping decreases: With B, BO 10 sts, knit to end.

Row 17 in neck-shaping increases: With B, CO 10 sts, knit to end.

SLEEVES

With B, CO 18 (24) sts.

Work 0 (4) rows in St st.

Rows 1–5: Beg with knit row, work in St st.

Row 6: P10, place removable marker, purl to end.

Rows 7–12: Change to A, work in St st.

Row 13: Change to B, join pleat with sts picked up to marker, remove marker, knit to end.

Rows 14 and 16: Purl.

Rows 15 and 17: CO 2 sts, knit to end.

Row 18: P15, place removable marker, purl to end.

Rows 19–24: Change to A, work in St st.

Row 25: Change to B, join pleat with sts picked up to marker, remove marker, knit to end.

Rows 26 and 28: Purl.

Rows 27 and 29: CO 2 sts, knit to end.

Row 30: P10, place removable marker, purl to end.

For Small
Rep rows 7–30 three times, and rep rows 7–12 once.

For Medium
Rep rows 7–30 three times, and rep rows 7–30 once with no incs.

For Both Sizes
Work 2nd half of sleeve. Start new row count.

Rows 1 and 2: With B, beg with knit row, work in St st.

Rows 3 and 5: Knit.

Row 4: Purl.

Row 6: P15, place removable marker, purl to end.

Rows 7–12: Change to A, work in St st.

Row 13: Change to B, join pleat with sts picked up to marker, remove marker, knit to end.

Rows 14 and 16: Purl.

Rows 15 and 17: BO 2 sts, knit to end.

Row 18: P10, place removable marker, purl to end.

Rows 19–24: Change to A, work in St st.

Row 25: Change to B, join pleat with sts picked up to marker, remove marker, knit to end.

Rows 26 and 28: Purl.

Rows 27 and 29: BO 2 sts, knit to end.

Row 30: P15, place removable marker, purl to end.

For Small
Rep rows 7–30 three times.

For Medium
Rep rows 7–30 once with no decs, rep rows 7–30 three times.

For Both Sizes:
Rep rows 7–12 once.

Next row: Change to B, join pleat with sts picked up to marker, remove marker, knit to end.

Work 5 (9) rows in St st.

BO all sts.

FINISHING

Sew tog shoulder and side seams, avoiding the pleats, leaving them to stand out at the seams. Sew in sleeves in the same way. Steam bottom sections of back, front, and sleeves.

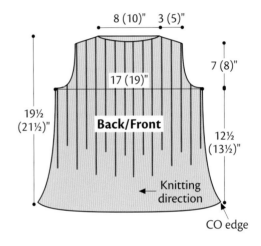

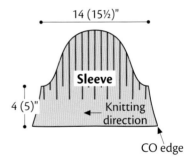

GRACE OF GRAYS:
Short-Row Pleats Pullover

Short-row pleats plus short-row shaping on the hips create
a classic silhouette. This piece is a challenge to make, but so easy
to dress up or down for any occasion.

Skill Level: Experienced ◼◼◼◼

Size: Small (Medium, Large)

Finished Bust Measurement: 36 (38, 40)"

Finished Back Length: 24 (25½, 27)"

MATERIALS

Zara from Filatura di Crosa (100% extra fine merino
superwash; 50 g/1.75 oz; 136 yds/125 m) 🧶

A 9 (10, 10) skeins in color 1914

B 2 skeins in color 1404

C 1 skein in color 1468

US 7 (4.5 mm) circular needle (24" long)

Spare US 4 (3.5 mm) circular needle to pick up
stitches

1 removable stitch marker

1 stitch marker

Size E-4 (3.5 mm) crochet hook

GAUGE

20 sts and 28 rows = 4" in St st

FEATURED TECHNIQUES

"Sectional Pleats in Stockinette Stitch" on page 9.

"Short Rows" on page 11.

Short-Row Pleats

Bottom pleats: The short-row pleats at hem
are worked in contrast color B as follows: With
A, knit to marker (placed in the previous row
to indicate beg of pleat), join B (do not cut A).
Work 10 rows of bottom pleat. The first row of
pleat continues the row that began with A. The
10th row of pleat begins the next WS row with
A. Cut B and purl to end of row with A.

Upper pleats: The short-row pleats at neck
are worked in contrast color B between two
rows of A. At right edge, join C (do not cut
A), work given number of sts, turn and work 9
rows of upper pleat. Cut B and work joining
pleat row with A.

BODY PLEAT PATTERNS
BOTTOM PLEAT
Worked over 40 (45, 50) sts.

Join B, do not cut A.

Row 1: K8 (9, 10), pm, knit to end.

Rows 2 and 3: Purl to marker, remove marker, turn
and wrap last st worked, K8 (9, 10), pm, knit to end.

Rows 4–9: Work rows 2 and 3 another 3 times.

Row 10: Purl, working wraps and wrapped sts tog.

UPPER PLEAT 1

Worked over 72 (74, 75) sts.

Join C, do not cut A.

Row 1: With C, knit to last 30 (35, 40) sts, turn.

Row 2: P15, pm, purl to end.

Rows 3 and 4: Knit to marker, remove marker, turn and wrap last st worked, P15, pm, purl to end.

Rows 5–10: Work rows 3 and 4 another 3 times.

UPPER PLEAT 2

Worked over 61 (63, 64) sts.

Join C, do not cut A.

Row 1: With C, knit to last 30 (35, 40) sts, turn.

Row 2: P15, pm, purl to end.

Rows 3 and 4: Knit to marker, remove marker, turn and wrap last st worked, P15, pm, purl to end.

Rows 5–10: Work rows 3 and 4 another 3 times.

BODY

Body is worked from side to side.

With A, CO 70 (75, 80) sts.

ARMHOLE AND SHOULDERS

Rows 1–5: Beg with knit row, work in St st.

Row 6: P40 (45, 50), place removable marker, purl to end.

Cont in St st, work bottom and upper pleats as indicated and AT SAME TIME inc 1 st at armhole edge in every row (K1f&b on RS, P1f&b on WS) 8 (10, 12) times.

Row 7 (inc): K1f&b, knit to marker, remove marker, join B (do not cut A), work bottom pleat.

Row 8 (inc): Complete bottom pleat rows, cut B, pick up A, purl to last st, P1f&b.

Row 9 (inc): K1f&b, knit to marker, join pleat with sts picked up from last row of A.

Rows 10 and 12 (inc): Purl to last st, P1f&b.

Rows 11 and 13 (inc): K1f&b, knit to end.

Cont in St st and work the following short rows to shape bottom of pullover, and AT SAME TIME work rem incs as needed for your size.

For Small

Rows 14 and 15: P40, turn and wrap last st worked, knit to end.

Row 16: Purl to wrapped st, purl wrap and wrapped st tog, purl to end.

Row 17: CO 24 sts, knit to end—102 sts.

Row 18: Purl.

Work 2 rows even.

For Medium

Rows 14 and 15: As rows 12 and 13.

Rows 16 and 17: P40, turn and wrap last st worked, knit to end.

Row 18: Purl to wrapped st, purl wrap and wrapped st tog, purl to end.

Row 19: CO 25 sts, knit to end—108 sts.

Work 4 rows, inc 1 st at beg of 3rd row for shoulder shaping.

For Large

Rows 14–17: Rep rows 12 and 13 twice.

Rows 18 and 19: P40, turn and wrap last st worked, knit to end.

Row 20: Purl to wrapped st, purl wrap and wrapped st tog, purl to end.

Row 21: CO 26 sts, knit to end—114 sts.

Work 6 rows, inc 1 st at beg of 5th row for shoulder shaping.

For All Sizes

Join C (do not cut A), work upper pleat 1.

Work 12 (14, 16) rows between upper pleat just completed and next bottom pleat as follows.

Start new row count.

Cont in St st and AT SAME TIME on row 7 (9, 11), K1, M1, knit to end.

Row 1: Cut C, with A join pleat with sts picked up on last row of A. Wrapped sts and wraps count as 1 st and are knitted tog with a st picked up. *Knit tog 1 st on main needle and 1 st on spare needle*; rep from * to * to wrapped st, place the wrap onto the left needle, knit tog wrap, wrapped st and corresponding st on spare needle**; rep from * to **.

Rows 2–7 (2–9, 2–11): Work in St st.

Rows 8 and 9 (10 and 11, 12 and 13): P40, turn and wrap last st worked, knit to end.

Rows 10–12 (12–14, 14–16): Work in St st.

Next bottom pleat.

Rows 13 and 14 (15 and 16, 17 and 18): Join B, work bottom pleat.

Work 12 (14, 16) rows between the bottom pleat and the next upper pleat as follows.

Cont in St st and AT SAME TIME on row 3 for all sizes, K1, M1, knit to end—104 (111, 117) sts.

Row 1: Cut B, with A join pleat with sts picked up on last row of A.

Rows 2 and 3 (2–5, 2–7): Work in St st.

Rows 4 and 5 (6 and 7, 8 and 9): P40, turn and wrap last st worked, knit to end.

Row 6 (8, 10): Purl.

Row 7 (9, 11): BO 8 sts, knit to end.

Row 8 (10, 12): Purl.

Row 9 (11, 13): BO 2 sts, knit to end.

Row 10 (12, 14): Purl.

Row 11 (13, 15): K2tog, knit to end.

Row 12 (14, 16): Purl.

Next upper pleat.

Rows 13 and 14 (15 and 16, 17 and 18): Join C, work upper pleat 2.

Work 12 (14, 16) rows between upper pleat just made and next bottom pleat as follows.

Row 1: Cut C, with A join pleat with sts picked up on last row of A. Wrapped sts and wraps count as 1 st and are knitted tog with a st picked up. *Knit tog 1 st on main needle and 1 st on spare needle*; rep from * to * to wrapped st, place the wrap onto the left needle, knit tog wrap, wrapped st and corresponding st on spare needle**; rep from * to **.

Rows 2–7 (2–9, 2–11): Work in St st and AT THE SAME TIME on rows 7 (9, 11), K2tog, knit to end.

Rows 8 and 9 (10 and 11, 12 and 13): P40, turn and wrap last st worked, knit to end.

Rows 10–12 (12–14, 14–16): Work in St st.

Next bottom pleat.

Rows 13 and 14 (15 and 16, 17 and 18): Join B, work bottom pleat.

Work 12 (14, 16) rows between last bottom pleat and next upper pleat as follows.

Start new row count.

Row 1: Cut B, with A join pleat with sts picked up on last row of A.

Rows 2 and 3 (2–5, 2–7): Work in St st.

Rows 4 and 5 (6 and 7, 8 and 9): P40, turn and wrap last st worked, knit to end.

Row 6 (8, 10): Purl.

Row 7 (9, 11): K1, M1, knit to end.

Row 8 (10, 12): Purl.

Row 9 (11, 13): K1, M1, knit to end.

Row 10 (12, 14): Purl.

Row 11 (13, 15): K1, M1, knit to end.

Row 12 (14, 16): Purl.

Next upper pleat.

Rows 13 and 14 (15 and 16, 17 and 18): Join C, work upper pleat 2.

Work 12 (14, 16) rows between last upper pleat and next bottom pleat as follows.

Start new row count.

Row 1: Cut C, with A join pleat with sts picked up on last row of A. Wrapped sts and wraps count as 1 st and are knitted tog with a st picked up. *Knit tog 1 st on main needle and 1 st on spare needle*; rep from * to * to wrapped st, place wrap onto left needle, knit tog wrap, wrapped st and corresponding st on spare needle**; rep from * to **.

Row 2: Purl.

Row 3: K1, M1, knit to end.

Row 4: Purl.

Row 5: CO 2 sts, knit to end.

Row 6: Purl.

Row 7: CO 8 sts, knit to end.

Work 0 (2, 4) rows even.

Rows 8 and 9 (10 and 11, 12 and 13): P40, turn and wrap last st worked, knit to end.

Rows 10–12 (12–14, 14–16): Work in St st.

Next bottom pleat.

Rows 13 and 14 (15 and 16, 17 and 18): Join B, work bottom pleat.

Work 12 (14, 16) rows between the last bottom pleat and the next upper pleat as follows.

Shape shoulder.

Start new row count.

Row 1: K2tog, knit to pleat, cut B, with A join pleat with sts picked up from last row of A.

Rows 2 and 3 (2–5, 2–7): Work in St st.

Rows 4 and 5 (6 and 7, 8 and 9): P40, turn and wrap last st worked, knit to end.

Row 6 (8, 10): Purl.

Row 7 (9, 11): K2tog, knit to end.

Rows 8–12 (10–14, 12–16): Work in St st.

Next upper pleat.

Rows 13 and 14 (15 and 16, 17 and 18): Join C, work upper pleat 1.

Work 12 (14, 16) rows between last upper pleat and next bottom pleat.

Shape shoulder and armhole.

Start new row count.

Row 1: Cut C, with A join pleat with sts picked up on last row of A. Wrapped sts and wraps count as 1 st and are knitted tog with a st picked up. *Knit tog 1 st on main needle and 1 st on spare needle*; rep from * to * to wrapped st, place the wrap onto the left needle, knit tog wrap, wrapped st and corresponding st on spare needle**; rep from * to **.

Row 2: Purl.

For Small
Row 3: BO 24 sts, knit to end.

For Medium
Row 3: K2tog, knit to end.

Row 4: Purl.

Row 5: BO 25 sts, knit to end.

For Large
Rows 3 and 4: Work in St st.

Row 5: K2tog, knit to end.

Row 6: Purl.

Row 7: BO 26 sts, knit to end.

For All Sizes
Rows 4–7 (6–9, 8–11): Work in St st and dec 1 st at beg and end of every row.

Rows 8 and 9 (10 and 11, 12 and 13): P40, turn and wrap last st worked, knit to end.

Rows 10–12 (12–14, 14–16): Work in St st and dec 1 st at beg and end of every row.

Next bottom pleat.

Rows 13 and 14 (15 and 16, 17 and 18): Join B, work bottom pleat, and dec 1 st at beg and end of each row.

Next row: K2tog, knit to pleat, cut B, with A join pleat with sts picked up from last row of A.

Work 5 rows in St st.

BO all sts.

BACK

Work as for front but omit neck shaping and work upper pleat 1 in place of working upper pleat 2 twice.

SLEEVE PLEAT PATTERNS
BOTTOM PLEAT
Worked over 40 (45, 50) sts.

Join B, do not cut A.

Row 1: K8 (9, 10), pm, knit to end.

Rows 2 and 3: Purl to marker, remove marker, turn and wrap, K8 (9, 10), pm, knit to end.

Rows 4–9: Work rows 2 and 3 another 3 times.

Row 10: Purl, working wraps and wrapped sts tog. Cut B.

UPPER PLEAT
Worked over 55 (60, 65) sts.

Join C, do not cut A.

Rows 1 and 2: K55, turn, P11 (12, 13), pm, purl to end.

Rows 3 and 4: Knit to marker, remove marker, turn and wrap last st worked, P11 (12, 13), pm, purl to end.

Rows 5–8: Work rows 3 and 4 another 2 times.

Rows 9 and 10: Knit to marker, remove marker, turn and wrap last st worked, purl to end. Cut C. Pick up sts with a spare needle to finish pleat.

SLEEVES

Worked from side to side, the sleeves are shaped with short rows, and decorated with two bottom pleats and one upper pleat.

With A and size 7 needle, CO 60 (65, 70) sts.

To shape underarm seam edge, work short rows as follows:

Rows 1 and 2: K12 (13, 14), turn and wrap last st worked, purl to end.

Rows 3 and 4: K24 (26, 28), turn and wrap last st worked, purl to end.

Rows 5 and 6: K36 (39, 42), turn and wrap last st worked, purl to end.

Rows 7 and 8: K48 (52, 56), turn and wrap last st worked, purl to end.

Row 9: K60 (65, 70), working wraps and wrapped sts tog as you come to them.

Row 10: Purl.

Work 0 (0, 2) rows in St st.

Cap shaping incs: K1f&b at beg of every RS row and P1f&b at beg of every WS row 25 (30, 35) times—85 (95, 105) sts.

Work 52 (54, 58) rows in St st to middle of sleeve and AT SAME TIME work incs for cap shaping and AT SAME TIME work bottom pleat in rows 37 and 38 (39 and 40, 42 and 42), and upper pleat in rows 51 and 52 (55 and 56, 59 and 60). Upper pleat is in middle of the sleeve.

Rows 53 (57, 61): Cut C, with A join pleat with sts picked up on last row of A. Wrapped sts and wraps count as 1 st and are knitted tog with a st picked up. *Knit tog 1 st on main needle and 1 st on spare needle*; rep from * to * to wrapped st, place the wrap onto left needle, knit tog wrap, wrapped st, and corresponding st on spare needle**; rep from * to **.

Work 17 (14, 11) rows even.

Cap shaping decs: K2tog at beg of every RS row and P2tog at beg of every WS row 25 (30, 35) times—60 (65, 70) sts.

Cont in St st and AT SAME TIME work decs for cap shaping and AT SAME TIME work bottom pleat in rows 73 and 74 (75 and 76, 77 and 78).

When all decs are completed, 60 (65, 70) sts on the needle, work 0 (0, 2) rows in St st. Then work short rows to shape underarm seam edge.

Rows 1 and 2: Knit to last 12 (13, 14) sts, turn and wrap last st worked, P12 (13, 14) sts, pm, purl to end.

Rows 3 and 4: Knit to marker, remove marker, turn and wrap last st worked, P12 (13, 14) sts, pm, purl to end.

Work rows 3 and 4 another 3 times.

BO all sts, working wraps and wrapped sts tog.

FINISHING

Steam finished pieces and let dry. Sew tog shoulders, but do not stitch through pleats. Sew sleeves into armholes. Sew sleeve and side seams together. With A and crochet hook, work a row of sc around bottom edge, neck edge, and, sleeve cuffs (do not stitch into pleats). Steam edges.

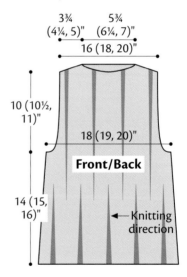

3¾ (4¼, 5)"   5¾ (6¼, 7)"
16 (18, 20)"
10 (10½, 11)"
18 (19, 20)"
Front/Back
14 (15, 16)"
←Knitting direction

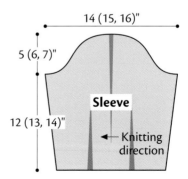

14 (15, 16)"
5 (6, 7)"
Sleeve
12 (13, 14)"
←Knitting direction

Abbreviations and Glossary

approx	approximately	PU	pick up and knit
beg	begin(ning)	pw	purlwise
BO	bind off	rem	remain(ing)
ch(s)	chain(s)	rep(s)	repeat(s)
CC	contrasting color	rev sc	reverse single crochet (also called crab stitch)
CO	cast on	rev St st(s)	reverse stockinette stitch(es)—purl on right side, knit on wrong side
cont	continue(ing)(s)		
dec	decrease(ing)(s)	rnd(s)	round(s)
dpn(s)	double-pointed needle(s)	RS	right side
inc(s)	increase(s) or increasing	sc	single crochet
K	knit	sl	slip
K1f&b	knit into front and back of same stitch—1 stitch increased (see page 12)	sl 1 pw	slip 1 stitch purlwise
		sl st(s)	slip stitch(es)
K2tog	knit 2 stitches together—1 stitch decreased (see page 12)	sm	slip marker
		ssk	slip 2 stitches knitwise, 1 at a time, to right needle, then insert left needle from left to right into front loops and knit 2 stitches together—1 stitch decreased (see page 12)
m	meter(s)		
M1	make 1 stitch—1 stitch increased (see page 12)		
		st(s)	stitch(es)
MB	make bobble	St st(s)	stockinette stitch(es)—in the round, knit every round; back and forth, knit on right side and purl on wrong side
MC	main color		
mm	millimeter(s)		
oz	ounce(s)		
P	purl	tbl	through back loop(s)
patt	pattern(s)	tog	together
P1f&b	purl into front and back of same stitch—1 stitch increased (see page 12)	WS	wrong side
		wyib	with yarn in back
P2tog	purl 2 stitches together—1 stitch decreased (see page 12)	yd(s)	yard(s)
		YO(s)	yarn over(s)
pm	place marker		

Resources

Contact the following companies to find shops that carry the fine yarns used in this book.

Alchemy Yarns of Transformation
www.alchemyyarns.com
Haiku
Synchronicity

Art Yarns
www.artyarns.com
Silk Rhapsody

Be Sweet
www.besweetproducts.com
African Bead Ball
Ribbon Ball

Blue Sky Alpacas
www.blueskyalpacas.com
Worsted Hand Dyes

Brown Sheep Company
www.brownsheep.com
Lamb's Pride Bulky

Classic Elite Yarns
www.classiceliteyarns.com
Lush

Dream in Color Yarn
www.dreamincoloryarn.com
Groovy

Filatura di Crosa
www.tahkistacycharles.com
Zara

Jacques Cartier Clothier
www.qiviuk.com

Vicuña

Karabella Yarns
www.karabellayarns.com
Gossamer

Malabrigo Yarn
www.malabrigoyarn.com
Twist

Mango Moon
www.mangomoonyarns.com
Elements

Prism Yarns
www.prismyarn.com
Angora
Tulle

Schulana/Skacel Collection
www.skacelknitting.com
Kid-Seta

Tilli Tomas/Planet Earth Fiber
www.tillitomas.com
Beaded Lace

Acknowledgments

I would first like to thank the late and much-missed Melissa Matthay. My love and thanks also go to Gina Wilde at Alchemy Yarns, and to my many knitting friends whom I first met through the Knitting Tree in Madison, Wisconsin: Jackie, Rhonda, Jean, Jo-Jo, Carmen, Ellen, and many others—you know who you are. I'm especially grateful to Sheryl Thies for useful advice regarding publishing matters, and to the various firms (listed elsewhere) who generously supplied materials.

My deepest gratitude goes to Mary Green and all the staff at Martingale & Company who helped me realize my designs and produce this beautiful book. I would particularly like to thank Ursula Reikes, my technical editor, for her invaluable assistance. Her meticulous work has significantly improved the final product. I would also like to thank my family and friends for their support and patience over the years, and Princess and Coco Chanel for their feline interest in my yarns and needles, and for much else besides.

There's More Online!

Find more exciting books on knitting, crochet, quilting, and more at www.martingale-pub.com.

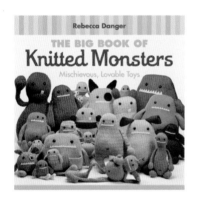

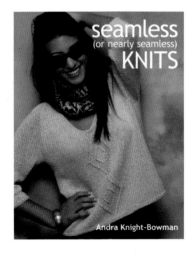